Multi-
Track
Diplomacy

Kumarian Press Books for a World that Works

Multi-Track Diplomacy:
A Systems Approach to Peace, Third Edition
Louise Diamond and John McDonald

The Immigration Debate: Remaking America
John Isbister

When Corporations Rule the World
David C. Korten

GAZA: Legacy of Occupation—A Photographer's Journey
Dick Doughty and Mohammed El Aydi

Bread, Bricks, and Belief:
Communites In Charge of Their Future
Mary Lean

HIV & AIDS: The Global Inter-Connection
Elizabeth Reid, editor

All Her Paths Are Peace:
Women Pioneers in Peacemaking
Michael Henderson

The Human Farm:
A Tale of Changing Lives and Changing Lands
Katie Smith

Summer in the Balkans:
Laughter and Tears after Communism
Randall Baker

Voices from the Amazon
Binka Le Breton

Multi-Track Diplomacy

A Systems Approach to Peace THIRD EDITION

Dr. Louise Diamond
Ambassador John McDonald

Kumarian Press

Kumarian Press Books for a World that Works

Multi-Track Diplomacy: A Systems Approach to Peace, Third Edition.

Published 1996 in the United States of America by Kumarian Press, Inc.,
14 Oakwood Avenue, West Hartford, Connecticut 06119-2127 USA.

Production supervised by Jenna Dixon
Copyedited by Linda Lotz   *Typeset by UltraGraphics*
Index prepared by Mary Neumann

Printed in the United States of America on recycled acid-free paper by
Thomson-Shore, Inc. Text printed with soy-based ink.

Library of Congress Cataloging-in-Publication Data
Diamond, Louise, 1944–
    Multi-track diplomacy : a systems approach to peace / Louise Diamond,
John McDonald. — 3rd ed.
        p.   cm. — (Kumarian Press books for a world that works)
    Includes bibliographical references and index.
    ISBN 1-56549-057-6 (paper : alk. paper)
    1. Peace. 2. Peace movements. I. McDonald, John W. 1922–
II. Title. III. Series.
JX1952.D525   1996
327.1'72—dc20   95-42452

05 04 03 02 01 00 99 98 97 96   10 9 8 7 6 5 4 3 2 1   1st Printing 1996

Dedication

In many cultures a significant action is always begun and ended with a dedication. We would like to dedicate this book, and whatever benefits may arise from it, to that wonderous peace pachyderm, the Multi-Track Diplomacy system, and to the realization of its collective vision of peace. May all our hopes and dreams for a peaceful world be furthered by the thoughts presented here, and may we all be strengthened by our efforts.

One Native American tradition says that if an action doesn't grow corn to feed the people, what good is it? We hope that this book will nourish and water the cornfields of peace, that citizens of this planet shall no longer hunger or thirst for a peaceful and fulfilling life.

Contents

Preface   viii

Introduction   1

The System as a Whole: Multi-Track Diplomacy   11

Track One   *   Government
Peacemaking through Diplomacy   26

Track Two   *   Nongovernment/Professional
*Peacemaking through Professional Conflict
Resolution*   37

Track Three   *   Business
Peacemaking through Commerce   52

Track Four   *   Private Citizen
Peacemaking through Personal Involvement   60

Track Five   *   Research, Training, and Education
Peacemaking through Learning   70

Track Six   *   Activism
Peacemaking through Advocacy   87

Track Seven   *   Religion
Peacemaking through Faith in Action   97

Track Eight   *   Funding
Peacemaking through Providing Resources   108

Track Nine   *   Communications and the Media
Peacemaking through Information   120

Preparing for a New Millenium: Issues Facing
the Multi-Track Diplomacy System   131

Intrasystemic Relationships   156

Recommendations   162

Bibliography   166

Index   175

Preface

The original research and writing of this book took place in 1991. Between that time and the present, there have been many changes in the world of international relations and in the Multi-Track Diplomacy system. The most significant change for us took place in 1992, with the establishment of the Institute for Multi-Track Diplomacy (IMTD).

We designed the IMTD intending to fulfill our own recommendations for establishing institutions that can take a systemic view of peacebuilding and conflict resolution. In fact, our projects in Cyprus, Israel and Palestine, Liberia, and elsewhere have been models of Multi-Track Diplomacy in action. Our work in these areas has brought people together for peacebuilding activities that not only span ethnic, religious, and national divides but also bridge the diverse interests of many (and in some cases all) of the nine tracks of the multi-track system. We have facilitated coordination and cross-pollination between the tracks and have participated in building alliances and consortia that engender cooperation among several sectors. In short, we have now seen this systems approach in action and can attest to its powerful effects.

Our goal in undertaking the study for this book was to present an overview of the field. Over one hundred personal interviews were conducted, supplemented by books, pamphlets, annual reports, and other materials from people and organizations in the nine tracks. Nine national and international conferences, which brought people together from within or among the tracks, were attended. For each person or organization studied, the topics considered included the mission, mandate, source of funds, structure, activities, products, results, difficulties, strengths, place in the field, future plans, and perceived effectiveness. In addition to the authors, eight volunteer part-time research assistants contributed to the gathering and analysis of information, and two other assistants helped put the manuscript together.

On a more personal note, we would like to acknowledge what is hard to represent in a formal study or on the printed page: the exquisite vitality of the individuals and the work in this field. The people interviewed represent an incredible diversity of values, perspectives, and modes of action; their work probes the very frontiers of our knowledge about how we can live together in peace on this planet.

This is a field that attracts exceptionally committed, creative, and caring individuals. For every person mentioned here, there are numerous others, unnamed and unheralded, who also are part of this vast and amazingly vital network, whose efforts hold such promise on a subject that is so important to the life of every single inhabitant of this planet. The numbers of involved individuals and institutions are growing year by year, and those interviewed were intrigued by the notion of seeing themselves as part of a larger system. We found the work thoroughly delightful and offer their reflections in that vein of joy.

We are grateful to the United States Institute of Peace for the grant that funded the research on which this book is based, and for its warm encouragement and support of the project.

We would also like to thank the many people who worked on the research and made this book possible:

- Students in Ron Pagnucco's Peace Studies class at Catholic University, who assisted with the research for class credit: Patricia Mulicka, Nancy McCarthy, Cindy Scroggins, and Kathleen Thoma;

- Christine Romero, who came as a student from Ron's class and stayed through the year, offering invaluable help and learning enough about Multi-Track Diplomacy to share it at a conference with her peers;

- Andrea Drongosky, Rebecca Youngman Forbes, and Leah Keder, who worked on various parts of the book as volunteer research assistants;

- Kevin Mutschler, who proofread the manuscript and offered last-minute, late-night typing help for the first edition;

- Jamie Notter, who helped with the editing and formatting for the second and third editions;

- Lynn Russillo, who helped put the thousands of little pieces together;

- Legacy International, which made special arrangements for researchers to attend one of its conferences;

- Dhyani Ywahoo, whose encouragement and inspiration were unfailing;

- All the interviewees, who are the very heart of this book; and

- All our friends and family, who encouraged and supported us unceasingly.

The views presented here are solely those of the authors and do not necessarily represent the views of the United States Institute of Peace.

Introduction

In understanding the system by which international peacemaking occurs, we might consider the parable of the blind man and the elephant. Like the blind man, if we feel only the trunk or the tusk or the tail of the peace pachyderm, we will misperceive the true nature of this lively creature. Likewise, if we consider the animal as a whole but don't know the parts and how they each contribute, we lose the value of acquaintance with a richly complex being.

Multi-Track Diplomacy is a conceptual way to view the process of international peacemaking in the United States as a whole elephant—that is, as a living system. It looks at that web of interconnected parts (activities, individuals, institutions, communities) that operate together, whether awkwardly or gracefully, for a common goal: a world at peace. The value of such a view is that it gives us a tool for self-examination and reflection. It enables us to see who we are, what we're doing, how we're doing it, where we're headed, and why.

The term *Multi-Track Diplomacy* refers to a conceptual framework we designed to reflect the variety of activities that contribute to international peacemaking and peacebuilding. The concept is an expansion of the "Track One, Track Two" paradigm that has defined the field during the last decade.

Historically, the notion of two tracks arose from the realization by diplomats, social scientists, conflict resolution professionals, and others that formal, official, government-to-government interactions between instructed representatives of sovereign nations were not necessarily the most effective methods for securing international cooperation or resolving differences or conflicts. The phrase "Track Two" was coined in 1982 by Joseph Montville of the Foreign Service Institute to describe methods of diplomacy that were outside the formal governmental system. It refers to nongovernmental, informal, and unofficial contacts and activities between private citizens or groups of individuals, sometimes called citizen diplomats or nonstate actors. These activities have three broad objectives:

1. To reduce or resolve conflict between groups or nations by improving communication, understanding, and relationships;

2. To decrease tension, anger, fear, or misunderstanding by humanizing the "face of the enemy" and giving people direct personal experience of one another; and

3. To affect the thinking and action of Track One by addressing root causes, feelings, and needs and by exploring diplomatic options without prejudice, thereby laying the groundwork for more formal negotiations or for reframing policies.

The basic premise of Track Two diplomacy, as it came to be understood in university, research, and practitioner circles in the 1980s, is that the expertise for dealing successfully with conflict and peacemaking does not reside solely within government personnel or procedures. Rather, citizens from a variety of backgrounds and with a variety of skills have something to offer and can make a difference.

This assumption has long been held by religious groups, which have historically had a strong local presence in areas of potential or actual conflict and have found an ever-increasing need and opportunity to use their established credibility and good offices to help mediate conflicts informally. Likewise, in the 1980s and 1990s, citizens from all walks of life—housewives, medical professionals, educators, scientists, and others—have come to understand the power of building personal relationships across "enemy" lines. Out of this has come the burgeoning citizen diplomacy movement. Private citizens have taken themselves in record numbers, individually and in groups, to the former Soviet Union, Central America, Israel and the Occupied Territories, Ireland, South Africa, and other places to "see for themselves" and to establish bonds of friendship and networks of mutual support and ongoing relationships.

While professionals and private citizens have been exploring their newfound power to make a difference, there has been a similar upsurge of interest in peace and world order in the education field. Several hundred colleges and universities now have programs in peace studies or conflict resolution, and there are increasing numbers of master's and Ph.D. programs in the field. Likewise, K–12 educators are designing global and peace studies units for their classrooms and conducting "peer mediation" courses. Building on the popularity of the alternative dispute resolution (ADR) movement, some are even enacting mediation programs with and for students.

Why has interest in nongovernmental diplomacy and the theory and practice of peacemaking grown so enormously? We suggest three possible answers. The first reflects the growing awareness—especially in light of the heightened consciousness of our worldwide environmental problems—that the planet is indeed an interdependent whole. People have begun to realize that the effects of their actions reach across national boundaries. As they have been able to witness, via television, the human faces of suffering from war, famine, and natural disaster, they have discovered that they want to, and can, do something to help.

Second, there has been a growing realization that the world is not structured to cope with most international conflicts. Wars between nations and conflicts between ethnic, religious, or political groups within nations have lasted for long periods and defied multiple and reasonable attempts at resolution: the Iran-Iraq war; the Afghan conflict; the Israeli-Arab situation; the Northern Ireland situation; the communal conflict between Hindus and Muslims in India; the years of violence in Nicaragua, Guatemala, El Salvador, Ethiopia, Sudan, and South Africa. These situations have infused the consciousness of a whole generation with the notion that we don't have the means to deal effectively with wars between sovereign states or, more common with the end of the Cold War, regional and ethnic conflicts between groups within states and across state lines.

The main formal mechanism for mediating world conflicts is the United Nations, but it has two serious constraints on its effectiveness: the Security Council is a political body with a veto option that allows the United States, the United Kingdom, Russia, France, or China to sidetrack discussion or action on any situation; and the UN Charter forbids the UN from intervening in what is euphemistically called "domestic affairs." No other international, reputable, reliable institution for peacemaking yet exists to cope with intrastate conflict.

In a vacuum, alternatives arise and people step forward. This stepping forward is fueled by a frustration that citizens feel when governments fail to be effective, innovative, and imaginative in dealing with long-standing problems, both at home and abroad. Along with this frustration comes a sense of empowerment—a thought that "if the leaders aren't doing it, let me try."

Finally, as deadly weapons find their way into the hands of groups and individuals all over the world, and as we recognize the potentially devastating effects of armed conflict anywhere, there is a renewed interest in the art and science of peace. When a single conflict could so easily lead to worldwide destruction—in other words, when faced with the issue of planetary survival—the forces for peace are mobilized.

For these and perhaps other less visible reasons, the nongovernmental movement toward peacemaking and peacebuilding has grown exponentially in recent years. As a result, we concluded that the designation of Track Two no longer covered the variety, scope, and depth of citizen involvement. We developed the concept of Multi-Track Diplomacy to begin the process of defining and describing the whole picture. Multi-Track Diplomacy consists of nine tracks in a conceptual and practical framework for understanding this complex system of peacemaking activities:

1. *Government, or Peacemaking through Diplomacy.* This is the world of official diplomacy, policymaking, and peacebuilding as expressed through formal aspects of the governmental process: the executive branch, the State Department, Congress, the U.S. Trade Representative's Office, the United Nations, and others.

2. *Nongovernment/Professional, or Peacemaking through Conflict Resolution.* This is the realm of professional nongovernmental action attempting to analyze, prevent, resolve, and manage international conflicts by nonstate actors.

3. *Business, or Peacemaking through Commerce.* This is the field of business and its actual and potential effects on peacebuilding through the provision of economic opportunities, international friendship and understanding, informal channels of communication, and support for other peacemaking activities.

4. *Private Citizen, or Peacemaking through Personal Involvement.* This includes the various ways that individual citizens become involved in peace and development activities through citizen diplomacy, exchange programs, private voluntary organizations, nongovernmental organizations, and special-interest groups.

5. *Research, Training, and Education, or Peacemaking through Learning.* This track includes three related worlds: research, as it is connected to university programs, think tanks, and special-interest research centers; training programs that seek to provide training in practitioner skills such as negotiation, mediation, conflict

resolution, and third-party facilitation; and education, including kindergarten through Ph.D. programs that cover various aspects of global or cross-cultural studies, peace and world order studies, and conflict analysis, management, and resolution.

6. *Activism, or Peacemaking through Advocacy.* This track covers the field of peace and environmental activism on such issues as disarmament, human rights, social and economic justice, and advocacy of special-interest groups regarding specific governmental policies.

7. *Religion, or Peacemaking through Faith in Action.* This examines the beliefs and peace-oriented actions of spiritual and religious communities and such morality-based movements as pacifism, sanctuary, and nonviolence.

8. *Funding, or Peacemaking through Providing Resources.* This refers to the funding community—those foundations and individual philanthropists that provide the financial support for many of the activities undertaken by the other tracks.

9. *Communications and the Media, or Peacemaking through Information.* This is the realm of the voice of the people: how public opinion gets shaped and expressed by the media—print, film, video, radio, electronic systems, the arts.

Each of these nine tracks represents a world unto itself, with its own philosophy and perspective, purpose, language, attitudes, activities, diversities, culture, and membership. At the same time, each of these worlds exists in the context of the others. Among and between these mini-worlds are numerous places of overlapping, collaborative, and complementary activities; relationships that span the spectrum from close and natural allies to adversaries; and varying degrees of openness for communication and mutual support. Therefore, the study of Multi-Track Diplomacy is more than simply a view into each of the tracks individually. It looks at the interrelatedness between them as well. It looks at the whole system.

Mode of Analysis: A Systems Overview

The simplest definition of a system is that it is a set of interrelated components, acting with a common purpose, that exchanges information and energy with its environment. This could apply equally to a home heating system (mechanical), the body's digestive system (biological), calculus (mathematical), the solar system (astronomical), nuclear fission (chemical), existentialism (philosophical), the Cold War (political), or a family (social). All these systems can be said to have the same general characteristics: a purpose or primary task; constituent parts that are simultaneously whole systems in themselves and subsystems of the larger whole; activities that affect the energy and information coming into the system so that they leave in a different state; boundaries that manage those exchanges and structures that organize those activities; some means of self-regulation and adaptation that allow them to change over time, with changing conditions; and an environment or an even larger suprasystem, which provides the context within which they operate.

Social systems have an additional quality that is missing from mechanical, chemical, philosophical, and other nonorganic systems. They have human consciousness, or the ability to actively and intentionally participate in the functioning and organization of the system. It is this consciousness that makes human systems so infinitely exciting and complex and so useful and appropriate to study. It is the intentionality of our individual and collective human behavior that shapes our social, political, and economic realities on this planet. How we think, what we value, what we believe, what we want and need, and what we choose to pursue determine how we organize our community, national, international, and transnational lives. In short, these factors create the world we live in, now and in the future.

The Persian Gulf War and its aftermath provide a graphic example of the role of consciousness or intentionality in the behavior of systems. Armed forces (military systems) wrought devastation and death upon human beings, animals, buildings, armaments, land, bodies of water, and oil wells as a result of a whole history of political relationships that culminated in choices made by a few individuals. These people made their choices based on their views of what they saw as real in the situation. That there is no one constant "reality" is clear from the fact that all parties saw the same set of circumstances differently and acted accordingly.

The whole world had occasion to watch the consummate war-making system in action at every level: its local, regional, national, and international political components in their intricate diplomatic dramas; its military components, both hardware (weapons) and software (the people, the process, the leadership), in graphic action; its psychological components of motivation, propaganda, and emotions; its economic components in terms of direct and indirect costs; its informational components, through the role of the media; its waste products, in the tragic plight of the refugees. Had different choices been made by a few individuals, the world might have watched a peacemaking system in action, with some of the same players but with altogether different activities and results.

This book seeks to provide a rudimentary systems analysis of the peacemaking system as it exists in the United States at a particular moment in time. We say rudimentary because the subject is a vast one that could profit from any number of such analyses. All would be different, because no analysis is purely objective. A social system is not a static thing, an object that we can turn this way and that and observe coolly and rationally, an equation that can be tested in the laboratory and produce the same analysis every time. A social system, like the people who make it up, is a shifting, complex web of people and processes, conscious and unconscious, whose every aspect is open to different interpretation.

Indeed, the very act of analyzing is a factor in the analysis, because the interpreters—the researchers—are themselves part of the system, with their own views and perspectives. Scientists have discovered that the act of watching is itself an intervention in the system that influences the processes under study. This is especially true in social systems, where the researchers are related in any number of ways to the people and activities being considered, and where the analysis itself (in this case the act of being interviewed) is an invitation for the actors to step back and consider themselves, something that an atom or a molecule in a laboratory test presumably cannot do.

These last two issues, of relationship and self-consciousness, stand out as perhaps the most significant. The first relates to content and the second to process, and if the reader goes no further than this section, he or she will have gleaned the heart of the wisdom this book has to offer.

Relationship is indeed the heart of the peacemaking system. Connectedness and interaction are what systems are all about. The nine tracks are related to one another as a whole system, operating on a web of personal relationships that extend across time and space, across age, gender, and national boundaries. We speak here not of hypothetical or potential relationships but of real-life personal connections, of networks, of the familiar "who do you know" routine by which things get done.

In a small town, an office, or a bureaucratic system, one expects things to operate through personal relations. We are living in a time when the world is called a "global village." Through the increased accessibility provided by telephones, television, fax, computers, E-mail, and airplanes, people in and out of formal leadership roles can develop and maintain close personal relations with others anywhere in the world. The vision of former President Bush on the phone with coalition leaders talking about strategies for dealing with the gulf crisis is an obvious example of such a network. What the research for this book uncovered, in every track, is that equally important networks exist throughout, among, and between every level of the system.

Landrum Bolling, for instance, a Track Two practitioner, began to work through the Quaker community to help the Arab-Israeli communication process nearly twenty-five years ago. In the course of that work he met Evgeny Primacov, now a prominent Russian leadership figure, and maintained an ongoing relationship with him over the years. When Bolling was asked to help address issues of human rights violations against religious practitioners in the USSR, he knew whom to call. An unofficial but high-level series of conferences resulted, culminating in the release of religious prisoners in the then Soviet Union and the rewriting of Soviet laws concerning religious freedom, in part with the help of American jurists.

As another example, in 1975, Alec Smith, son of Prime Minister Ian Smith of Rhodesia (now Zimbabwe), met and befriended black nationalist leader Arthur Konoderkeka at a Moral Re-Armament conference in Rhodesia. Their ensuing friendship eventually led to a meeting between Robert Mugabe and Ian Smith on the night before the announcement of Mugabe's victory in the Zimbabwean elections. As a result, a coup planned by the Rhodesian military was called off, and both Mugabe and Smith made reconciliatory statements to their constituencies, which assisted in the relatively peaceful turnover of power to black majority rule in Zimbabwe.

If relationship is the key to the substance of the peacemaking system of Multi-Track Diplomacy, self-consciousness is the key to its process. At a recent meeting of Track Two professionals, the participants were invited to answer a series of questions having to do with their values, their personal intentions and assumptions, and their modes of self-care in light of the high stress of their work. One member was overheard to say, with some wonderment, "But we never talk about these things!" For many, that part of the discussion was more highly energized than all the ensuing talk about theories of negotiation or other substantive issues. Several people reported that they have since changed their lives and work in various ways as a direct result of that self-examination.

When people stop to examine what they are doing, how they are doing it, why they are doing it, what they hope will come out of it, and what is helping or hindering them from achieving their goals, they are effectuating the most powerful tool of self-regulation available to a social system. The environment is always providing feedback to a system: how its products sell helps a business improve its production, promotion, and distribution modes; how its students fare in the job market helps a university determine its curriculum. The power of feedback from within the system is of equal if not greater value than that from the outside, for it involves a self-consciousness that builds awareness, and awareness is the first step in any change process.

This systems analysis is an attempt to increase the self-awareness of the peacemaking system so that it can consciously choose new directions, new behaviors, or new perspectives that will help it move into the twenty-first century as a more effective force for a far more peaceful millennium than the previous two. It is presented both as a study tool for reflection on the system and as a guidebook for those who wish to pursue these activities. The material is organized to provide a blueprint for individuals or groups that are asking themselves about their own work and its place in the field.

This book addresses the activities in each of the nine tracks and their interactions in the system as a whole. For the system as a whole and for each of its constituent tracks, we consider the purpose, which includes its primary task and the assumptions or worldview on which that task is based; the constituent parts, which we call *Shape of the Field*; the *Activities* in which those parts engage; and the means of self-regulation, which we call *Issues in the Field*. In addition, we examine a characteristic applicable to human systems, called *Culture*, to consider the norms, values, and characteristics of the part under discussion. Finally, we address the environment, which we call *Place in the Field*.

If we look at a system as a complex organism, like a family, we see that the different parts play different roles for the whole. That is, one component may play the leadership role, another the caretaking role, another the inspirational role. All these functions are necessary for a social system to be whole. In the *Place in the Field* sections, we consider the systemic role played by each track. We also consider its negative and positive potentials, for human beings have the capacity to use their gifts for harm or for good.

Following the description of each track is a resource list. These lists are not comprehensive. They include those individuals and institutions that were interviewed during the research, those that sent printed information on request, and those that were added during later revisions. Many that should be included are not represented here, simply because of time and space limitations.

Finally, we draw conclusions about issues common to the whole system and their implications for a new millennium, and we look at the intrasystemic relationships between the tracks. We conclude by making recommendations about what everyone involved in the Multi-Track Diplomacy system can do to strengthen it and the peacemaking process.

The System as a Whole
Multi-Track Diplomacy

The purpose of the Multi-Track Diplomacy system is to help the world become a more peaceful place, but this is not necessarily the primary task of each of the components. For instance, international business has as its primary goal financial success, and the media have as their objective to inform the public. In this book, however, we are addressing those streams within the nine fields that are specifically geared to, or at least related to, promoting peace.

To understand this purpose fully, we must address what some of the key words mean. For instance, why is the word *diplomacy* used to name the whole system? The term is commonly applied to Track One, the official interactions between governments, and is sometimes associated with activities in Track Two (unofficial diplomacy) or Track Four (citizen diplomacy), but it is rarely used in connection with business, the media, or academia. Using the word systemically can create cognitive dissonance, which can be a useful tool for learning. In those moments when we are challenged to see an old friend in new clothes, we must stretch beyond old habits and, in doing so, perhaps become more open to creative ways of thinking.

Diplomacy is also used to define this system because it is essentially about a process that Smith Simpson, retired U.S. diplomat, sees as "our principal means of tackling international problems and stabilizing a world precariously balanced between order and violence."[1] The actions that arise from each of the nine tracks are attempts at just that—at solving problems and finding a way through the miasma of violence to a just and peaceful world order.

Additionally, because *diplomacy* is associated in our minds with an interactive process, a back-and-forth between various parties, it is about relationship, communication, connectedness. These are the key elements not only of peacemaking endeavors but also of social systems. If the term jiggles the mind to associate the system with these efforts and qualities it will be relevant.

Another term needing definition is the word *peace* itself, central to the concept of Multi-Track Diplomacy as a system of peacemaking. The word has numerous definitions and a wide range of emotive connotations. That it means different things to different people can be illustrated by two events that happened to us.

In one, a businessman shared his perceptions of why the word *peace* had such low credibility in the business community and among his peers. He said that his generation, having lived through World War II, associated war with bringing about peace. They had some positive associations with soldiering and fighting that related not so much to the experience itself, which was awful, but to the necessity of doing so and the success of that war in stopping a mad tyrant and establishing a worldwide political basis for peace. When the children of those men and women protested the Vietnam War, adopting the peace sign and symbol as their identity badges, in the process they denounced soldiers and the very act of war, repudiating the truth of their parents' experience. The word *peace*, then, took on unpleasant associations for many, as it became linked to the anger and divisions of the 1960s.

In another instance, a religious group commended one of us for his advocacy of peace, which the group interpreted as meaning that he was a complete pacifist. Since members of the group used the terms interchangeably, they assumed that he would also.

Peace has been variously defined not just by connotative associations but also by whether it refers to an active process or a passive state. The term *negative peace* has come to mean the absence of war; *positive peace* includes concerns for social and economic justice, environmental integrity, human rights, and development. Betty Reardon, in a booklet published by the Five College Program in Peace and World Security Studies, elaborates:

> *Negative peace*, focusing on the present and near-future, implies the prevention and eradication of large-scale organized violence (i.e., war). This concept emphasizes the development of local, national, and global systems which foster the avoidance and resolution of conflicts by nonviolent means. A principal aim of such endeavors is to reduce the potential for military conflict through arms control and disarmament. . . .
>
> The concept of *positive peace* emerges from the belief that mere intervals between outbreaks of warfare do not constitute the true

opposite of war or violence, and that a second, more permanent approach to peace is therefore essential. This approach calls for the eradication of militarism (that is, the permanent mobilization of society for war) and of what is termed structural violence (that is, the brutalizing and often lethal effects of oppressive social systems). Positive peace is generally understood to entail a re-ordering of global priorities so as to promote social justice, economic development, and participatory political processes. This attention to structural issues is motivated both by an understanding that poverty and oppression are a primary cause of violence and war, and by a desire to construct a more humane world future.[2]

We have taken the wider definition of *positive peace* as the focus for purposes of this book, although activities seeking to stop and avoid war are also critical in the development of a more just and humane world and have been considered as well.

The word *peacemaking* also needs explanation. The term is used here generically rather than specifically. It refers not only to the concrete activities required to make peace between opposing parties but also to the whole range of behaviors that contribute to the prevention, management, and resolution of conflicts; to reconciliation and healing; to the exploration of issues related to the nature of peace and conflict in general and to specific conflicts or types of conflicts; to education and research about such issues; to theory building and direct practice; to influencing policy; to providing information; to facilitating dialogue, negotiation, and mediation; and to all those activities that lay the foundation for better trust and understanding and improved living conditions to ensure better relations among peoples and nations. In short, *peacemaking* here is used as shorthand to include all activities of what might otherwise be categorized as peacekeeping, peacebuilding, peace research, peace studies, peace education, and conflict resolution.

Finally, a word on *primary task*. Every system has a clear task; in fact, its effectiveness is measured by how strongly all the parts of the system are aligned with the task and how well they work together to fulfill their mission. Peace is not, however, a measurable commodity. It is a potential, a possibility, an ever-changing condition. A world at peace is not an objective to be accomplished by a certain date but a vision, a direction in which to head, one step at a time.

Correspondingly, it is virtually impossible to determine the effectiveness of any one action, event, document, or meeting or even a whole series of activities in creating a more peaceful world. Although this system has a clear task, it often operates in the dark, or at least the dusk—planting seeds here and there, watering them now and then, feeding them this way and that, hoping that the combined efforts, over time, will have lasting effects.

A curious note about the Multi-Track Diplomacy system is that it does not define itself as a system. That is, although the nine component subsystems might define their tasks similarly, and might even recognize that their work is related to the work of some of the other tracks, it is unlikely that most individuals or institutions within the system actually see themselves as part of the larger whole. So even though the components may share a common purpose, they may not be aware of working together to achieve that purpose. It is one of the basic contentions of this book that the very act of naming the system invites that self-definition and has the potential to lead to a greater conscious cooperation among the tracks.

Shape of the Field

The constituent parts of the system, the nine tracks, have been named and are now presented in graphic form (Figure 1). Each track occupies a unique position in the diagram, yet they are all connected by the outer circle and at the center. Track Nine is represented by the inner circle and links all the tracks together through its function, communication. The nine tracks are organized in a circle to suggest graphically the underlying principle of systemic thinking: the whole is greater than the sum of its parts. The components of this system are vastly different from one another, yet somehow they are sufficiently related to, and interactive with, one another to build a synergistic energy that carries their efforts beyond simple listing or summation of one plus one.

Whereas a circle can show the general shape, other forms can demonstrate the reorganization of the same components in functional rather than descriptive terms. One way of looking at the field is in the triangle of peace research, action, and education (Figure 2). In this model, discussed at the International Conference of Peace Institutes in Des Moines, Iowa, in June 1990, the system is defined by types of activities. Research includes both basic or pure research and applied or action research. Action includes advocacy and direct peacemaking; education refers to both informational and learning-by-doing activities. Although the three are consumers and resources for one another, they are also affecting and affected by the central

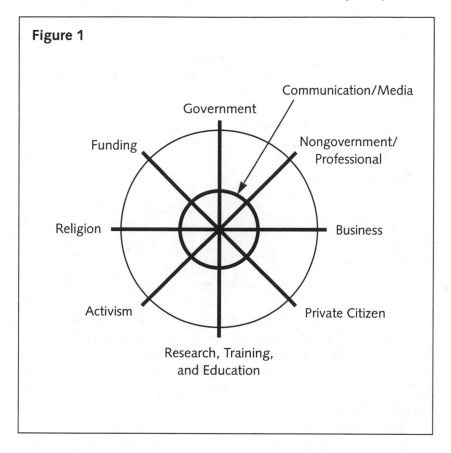

Figure 1

Communication/Media
Government
Funding
Nongovernment/
Professional
Religion
Business
Activism
Private Citizen
Research, Training,
and Education

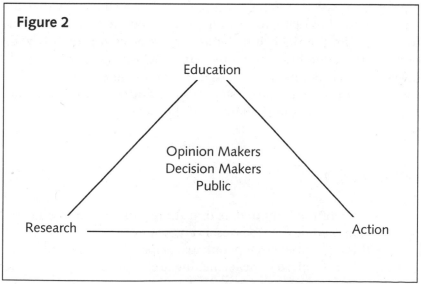

Figure 2

Education

Opinion Makers
Decision Makers
Public

Research — Action

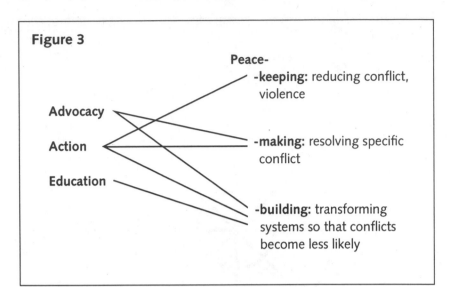

Figure 3

group: the public, its leaders, and those who shape its opinions. The relevant question with this model is, how does all this work together to produce good decisions that meet the needs of the people?

Another way of organizing by function is to consider the distinctions between peacemaking, peacebuilding, and peacekeeping. These categories can then be overlaid with types of behaviors to get a different model (Figure 3), which was presented at the same conference.

All these schema are useful. They show the richness and complexity of the system and the multiple ways in which its activities can be understood to relate to one another. Often individuals or institutions within the field find themselves associated primarily with one or another of these functions, but in fact they are involved with several at once. Sometimes it is useful for these lines to be blurred; sometimes they need to be crystal sharp. Living with this variety and ambiguity is one of the challenges of the field.

Culture

The diversity of the field means that there is little shared culture. Some commonalities can be observed, however.

First, this is not a field that people participate in to amass personal wealth. People involved in peacemaking are likely to act out of some value, some commitment to an ideal. This is more articulated in some subsystems than in others. The religious and activist communities, for instance, speak openly of their values and can imbue that talk with great passion. The academic and professional sectors tend to be more circumscribed in sharing their feelings or ideals and speak in more logical and rational terms, without acknowledging personal invest-ment. In spite of these differences in style, we did not meet a single individual or encounter a single institution in this field that was not engaged in some commitment to service, that did not have some motivation to work toward a reality derived from some positive ideal, even when that work involved great stress.

That stress, or distress, is another common factor. Conflict gener-ates suffering; suffering generates conflict. Because people in the peacemaking field are always dealing in some way with conflict or its potential, they are either directly or indirectly involved with issues of tremendous human pain and anguish. For those on the front lines day after day—like the human rights or international development groups or the religious field-workers—the pain can be overwhelm-ing. For those who drop into war zones, refugee camps, and impov-erished areas—the citizen diplomats, journalists, activists, conflict resolution facilitators, for instance—the shock can be devastating. Even for those who are shielded from the direct experience of the suffering—the diplomats, academics, funders, businesspeople—the information that they're dealing with and the sense of urgency, hope-lessness, and, occasionally, crisis, can generate great distress.

How the system deals with this stress remains one of the critical unanswered questions raised in this book. When some profession-als were asked that question, they first went blank, as if to say, "Oh, right, I guess I don't deal with it very consciously." Yet we know that stress inevitably takes its toll on their physical, emotional, and spiri-tual well-being in any number of ways.

It may be, too, that distance from the suffering is a factor in the system. During the course of completing the research for this book, two separate but similar articles appeared in the media. One described a visit by then Prime Minister de Klerk to a hostel in one of the black townships of South Africa where there had been heavy factional violence. Another mentioned a visit by a top State Department offi-cial to a Palestinian refugee camp in the occupied territories. For both men, these visits were their first personal experiences of such environments, and they were reportedly deeply moved. The shape of world events might be quite different if all decision makers were regularly exposed to the daily realities of the people about whom they make major decisions.

Another noticeable factor in the culture of this system is its fragmentation. All nine tracks are worlds unto themselves, with their own rules, languages, norms, and beliefs. Each tends to act as if it alone holds the key to world peace. This sense of "we know what's right" can encourage a disparagement of the others—a mode of "if only they would listen to us." Even when this self-focus does not result in any active negation of the others, it produces subtle barriers to communication and collaboration by, at the very least, the lack of pathways for shared effort.

Related to this fragmentation is the cliquishness that is found in most social systems. In each of the nine tracks and between and among them, there are "in" subgroups with more prestige and influence and "out" groups with less. This has the usual effect of depriving the whole system of some of the valuable resources of the "outs," and it encourages the norm of power through association. Credibility becomes an important issue and is associated to a high degree with one's institutional base or professional contacts. Although this cliquishness is more pronounced in certain parts of the system— for instance, the worlds of official diplomacy, conflict resolution professionals, and the academic and funding communities—it permeates the system, since these are the tracks that have the greatest power in setting and financing the agenda and determining the direction for the whole.

Activities

The range of activities within this system is vast and is described in the chapters covering the nine tracks. Of interest here is the paucity of structures and activities that relate to the system as a whole. We attribute this to the fact that the system is in the early stages of recognizing itself as a system. No systemic services have arisen as yet to manage and serve the whole.

Several institutions are broadly based, even if they do not cover all nine tracks. The United States Institute of Peace, for instance, though established and funded by the U.S. government, is not an integral part of the Track One structure that authorized it and must deal with its governmental parent the same way other think tanks or interest groups might. Being an official arm of the government, it deemphasizes relations with the activist and religious communities and is barred by law from involving itself in policymaking activities. However, it supports and encourages a wide range of research, education, and other activities that involve agents from several of the nine tracks.

Two other organizations that can be said to serve the field generally are the Consortium on Peace Research, Education and Development (COPRED) and the National Conference of Peace Making and Conflict Resolution (NCPCR). These two draw membership (in the former) and participants (in the latter) from many dimensions of the system and offer at their conferences some opportunities for the system to look at itself. Even here, however, some subsystems are more involved than others. The government, media, business, and funding communities are rarely represented at these conferences, which is perhaps a realistic view of the configuration of intrasystemic relationships.

Other organizations, notably the Peace Studies Association, the International Studies Association, the International Society of Political Psychology, the Society of Professionals in Dispute Resolution, and the International Peace Research Association, may have members from a number of tracks and take a multidisciplinary approach. Yet such organizations have specific and primary focuses and cannot be said to be systemic organizations whose job is to serve the entire field.

In terms of projects, too, very few have undertaken an overview of the whole field. The World Without War Council devised a topology to examine the slightly broader field of the U.S. role in world affairs and published a book on that subject.[3] Its focus was not peacemaking, per se, though the topology was remarkably similar to that of Multi-Track Diplomacy. No other project that we are aware of has attempted a similar effort.

Issues in the Field

This topic is perhaps best left to the final chapters of this book, after we have had an opportunity to review the issues that emerge from each of the nine tracks and make some sense of their systemic implications. What can be said here, however, is that there is indeed little conscious self-regulation in the Multi-Track Diplomacy system as a whole because there is little self-identification with the larger system by its constituent parts, and no institutions are in place to manage its care and encourage its development.

Place in the Field

The Multi-Track Diplomacy system, or the U.S. system involved with international peacemaking, exists in two important proximal (or close-by) environments and one distal (or more distant) context that are critical to its definition, its activities, and its success.

Proximally, the peacemaking system is intimately interconnected with the war-making system. Many of the major actors are the same: the UN Security Council, the president and his entire diplomatic and foreign policy apparatus, congressional leadership and committees, public opinion, the media, the religious community, and activists. The Persian Gulf War provided a graphic example of this overlap. Leading up to and during that war, individuals from all these groups appeared daily on television screens and their opinions were printed in the pages of newspapers and magazines. Academic experts and think tank specialists filled the talk shows. Citizen diplomats and conflict resolution specialists undertook various behind-the-scenes missions. American businesses with interest or expertise in Middle Eastern affairs became actively engaged. Even the military, which played a critical role in the conflict, was originally positioned to preserve the peace. War, too, is a multi-track endeavor and, at least in this country in the last century, has been invoked as a path to peace.

The relationship is a delicate one to describe. One view is that the war-making system kicks in when the peacemaking system fails or is not fully activated or encouraged, as was the case with the Persian Gulf War. It may also make sense to say that the two are reflective of each other. Dealing with interlocking conditions and actors, they nevertheless are activated by different intentions and beliefs, generate different activities, and produce different results. The peacemaking system operates on the same issues as its counterpart, which are issues of conflict between nations or identity groups, so it is always overlapping and interpenetrating the war-making system.

War and peace are inherently possible within each other. Perhaps it is the very tug of the two as played out by the individuals and institutions within these systems that determines actual events. In any event, it is clear that the two are related in some way, through an uneasy, sometimes adversarial partnership that provides an immediate and looming challenge for the peacemaking community.

The other proximal suprasystem is the international political order. The United States' involvement in the world's conflicts takes place on a complex field of formal and informal political, economic, legal, and social structures and realities that inform, constrain, and shape its actions. UN structures, regional security groups, economic conditions, historical legacies, factional politics, and religious, ethnic, and national strivings are ingredients in a huge pot of stew that the peacemaking community is always stirring. In this regard the system finds itself dealing with conditions not of its own making that it must relate to and interact with, seeking paths through the labyrinth in order to offer help without creating further harm.

In a systems view, the U.S. peacemaking complex of Multi-Track Diplomacy is but one subsystem of this larger whole. Its role in the greater scheme must be left to some other study. What is evident here is that the relationship between the U.S. peacemaking system and the international political order plays a central role in the workings of the system under study; it is the context in which most of its activities take place and by which they are given form and direction.

The more distal suprasystem, which we might term *world conditions*, is not less important for being more remote. In fact, we posit that present world conditions give the Multi-Track Diplomacy community its greatest opportunity and its most urgent challenge.

The world is changing rapidly, and the changes are not superficial. They affect not just the shape and quality of life on this planet but also the earth's very survival. These changes are of the same historical magnitude as the Industrial Revolution; they are capable of transforming the worldview and thereby the values, structures, and behaviors that will eventually determine and shape the daily lives of every being on this earth. The simplest way to describe these changes is to say that the world is recognizing its interdependence.

Although science has long recognized the interrelatedness of phenomena, the first major clue for the general public was the earliest set of photographs of the earth taken from outer space. Able to see ourselves from the outside, with national boundaries erased by distance and the poetic dance of wind and sea currents upon the fluid geometry of the land, we began to realize that we share something in common with one another despite the appearance of our profound differences, and that what we share might be more important than what we disagree about.

The rapid revolution in communications technology has added to this realization; we now have the means to be instantaneously visible and audible to one another virtually anywhere on the globe. This has produced what some call the global village phenomenon, meaning that the world has shrunk to the size of a village in terms of our ability to know, to see, to share. Through satellite hookups, we can visit with strangers as if they were in our living room; through computer and television networks, multilateral conferences can be held across continents. We can watch a child starve in Ethiopia, a mortar shell land in Sarajevo, or an earthquake ravage San Francisco as if it were happening in our front yard. This ability has given us access to new and rapid information and has broken down stereotypes and psychological boundaries about "the other" or "the enemy." In making the strange familiar, we have become embedded in one another's lives and dramas in a way that is unprecedented in history.

Then came our increased consciousness of environmental issues, and we began to realize that even small and seemingly insignificant events that happen in one place can have a major impact on people far away. With concerns about the ozone layer, pollution of the oceans, global warming, acid rain, deforestation, and other environmental threats coming to the forefront, we saw that the problems facing the world are not tied in neat little packages with one country's name on them. They are solvable only across national boundaries, through multilateral diplomacy, and with massive cooperation. They are indeed threats to our survival, every bit as much as nuclear war would be.

Global interdependence is becoming increasingly clear in other realms as well. No longer can we pretend that our economic health rests with us alone, that AIDS stops at national boundaries, or that the drug trade recognizes borders. No longer can we imagine that economic disaster in Mexico, political unrest in Ukraine, population growth in Pakistan, or changes in the ice conditions in Antarctica have nothing to do with our lives here in the United States. We are all related to and dependent on one another, and our well-being and survival require a new way of thinking about international relations.

Politically, the changes are evident in a number of ways. With the collapse of the Berlin Wall in November 1989 and the falling away of superpower rivalry, we are discovering that North-South disparities in resources and living standards may structure our international challenges more than East-West ideological conflicts. We are seeing that creative security and new political and economic structures are desperately needed to meet the needs of Eastern Europe, Central America, Africa, and other areas where old forms are breaking down and new forms have not fully emerged. We are finding that world order is threatened not so much by conflicts between nations but by conflicts among ethnic, religious, nationalist, and tribal identity groups. Their fights are not over interests such as boundaries or resources, which are negotiable; they are about existence, identity, language, culture, religion, and recognition—needs that are nonnegotiable.

Harold Saunders, director of international affairs at the Kettering Foundation and former State Department official, observes:

> More and more problems confront nations that no one nation can deal with by itself. Only by cooperating can nations deal adequately with them. This is true partly because these problems cut across national borders—nations are interdependent—and partly because there are more centers of influence today that affect events—the world is multipolar.[4]

He goes on to say that there is a "broadening participation of people, both in the governance of nations and in the relationships between nations," that "people feel they must harness their own political power in new ways to tackle chronic social and political problems" and are doing so by "thinking about politics in creative, non-institutional ways." Finally, he posits that, given these changes, "traditional instruments of statecraft often do not reliably accomplish what is expected of them."[5]

These changes have enormous implications for our political structures. The whole worldview of the last several centuries, which saw the nation-state as the unit of power and the balance of power as the principle of order, is no longer satisfactory to explain all the new conditions and forces at work in the world community. A new worldview is in the slow process of arising from our collective consciousness and our global experience. This view encompasses issues of interdependence and cooperation rather than dominance; of true collective security in which the collective includes the whole and not just the elite parts; of identity groups (tribal, religious, ethnic, racial, nationalistic) as well as national entities as the locus of power; of economic systems that meet the real needs of all people; of methods of relating to differences creatively; of resolving conflicts and solving problems without violence.

This new worldview will indeed give birth to a "new world order," though it may not look exactly like former President George Bush envisioned it. What we see as truth, how we explain the reality of our experience, determines how we act and how we treat one another; it determines the structures we build to order our lives and the values with which our actions are imbued.

Meanwhile, we stand, according to Saunders, "on the bridge between two paradigms," and standing there:

> We would be unwise not to act in recognition of elements of the future that are already with us and not to begin developing a world view that will enable us to act creatively in that future while we go on dealing with the present. When old pictures blur and old tools do not always work, the time comes to say "enough" and to search out more effective ways of thinking and acting.[6]

We believe that the world does indeed stand on that bridge between two ways of understanding our shared reality, and that the Multi-Track Diplomacy system is both a result of and an active agent for the immense transformational moment we face. The same force that brought people out in the streets in Eastern Europe to overthrow political systems that failed to meet their needs is here bringing people into the arena of citizen diplomacy, into the academic programs of peace studies and conflict resolution. The same view that allows us to see the world as one interdependent whole enables us to view the field of peacemaking as an extended system, with one goal achieved through many means.

It is the people and the institutions in the Multi-Track Diplomacy system that are taking up the challenge of developing the new political structures and relationship models that are needed to meet the needs of these changing times. This system, in its attempt to develop theoretical and practical means for making and keeping peace, is on the leading edge, the vanguard of human development. Quite simply, if we cannot learn to live together on this one earth peacefully, then we will suffer and ultimately die together, violently.

This is the context in which the Multi-Track Diplomacy system exists, to which it is always referent, and from which it draws its impetus and meaning. Standing between two worlds, every step we take in the present either breaks down or reinforces old patterns from the past and plants seeds for the future. As we proceed through the next several chapters to look carefully at each of the nine tracks, we will be reflecting back on this awareness.

Notes

1. Smith Simpson, *Perspectives on the Study of Diplomacy* (Washington, DC: Institute for the Study of Diplomacy, Georgetown University, 1986), p. 1.

2. Five College Program in Peace and World Security Studies, *Guide to Careers, Internships, and Graduate Education in Peace Studies* (Amherst, MA: Peace and World Security Studies, 1990), p. 4.

3. *Americans and World Affairs: A Guide to Organizations and Institutions in Northern California* (Berkeley, CA: World Without War Council of Northern California, 1988).

4. Harold H. Saunders, "The Politics of the Peace Process in a Global Perspective," 1990 epilogue to *The Other Walls: The Politics of the Arab-Israeli Peace Process* (Washington, DC: American Enterprise Institute for Public Policy Research, 1985), p. 3.

5. Saunders, pp. 4, 5, 7.

6. Saunders, p. 8.

Track One: Government
Peacemaking through Diplomacy

Diplomacy is a peaceful political process between nation-states that seeks to structure, shape, and manage over time a system of international relationships to secure a nation's interests. Utilized in the pursuit of many kinds of objectives—political, economic, national, trade, aid, human rights, arms control, scientific, cultural, and academic enrichment—diplomacy is both a peacebuilding and a peacemaking activity. It works at the government level to enhance trust, confidence, and understanding among nations as well as to provide negotiation, mediation, crisis intervention, and conflict resolution; it also seeks to prevent war.

Since the rise of the nation-state, the basic assumption of international diplomacy has been the notion of relative power. In power politics, stronger nations use coercion, leverage, threat, control of resources, rewards, punishments, and force of arms to influence or control weaker nations. Since maintaining power ascendancy may ultimately require armed might, the need to find ways to avert, prevent, manage, and resolve armed conflicts is woven into the fabric of geopolitical relations.

In this process, it is the nation itself, or its government, that is the vehicle of power. Thus we have developed an international system of relationships based primarily on the nation-state. Peoples; cultures; religious, ethnic, or political identity groups; and private citizens have no formal standing in the present global system.

Given the fact of global interdependence and the rise in importance of identity groups, these assumptions and the structures and procedures they spawn must change in the next century and become more focused on managing and nourishing mutually beneficial, ongoing relationships between people at every level of social organization.

26

Shape of the Field

The diplomatic community is the most clearly defined of the nine tracks. Because Track One refers to official governmental actions, the field is bounded by those elements of official government that engage in peacemaking activities. For the purposes of this book, we consider only certain key institutions within the U.S. government that are most actively engaged in making and implementing foreign policy: the State Department, the president and his national security apparatus, Congress, and related bodies such as the Office of the U.S. Trade Representative. Clearly other governmental bodies are relevant as well: the Defense Department, the Arms Control and Disarmament Agency, the Central Intelligence Agency, the U.S. Information Agency, the U.S. Agency for International Development, and the Departments of Commerce, Agriculture, and Labor, to name a few, are all players in the international arena, but their involvement must be left to another study.

This book also includes, in a rudimentary way, the United Nations. Although the scope of this book is limited to U.S. systems of peacemaking, the United Nations, being on U.S. territory and an important part of our foreign policy, is an integral part of this nation's diplomatic world.

Culture

The diplomatic world is both political and bureaucratic. For this reason, it has a highly heterogeneous culture. Language is formal, filled with acronyms and bureaucratic jargon. The dress code is rigid. This is a culture not about individual expression but about group norms.

In this world, loyalty and conformity are valued; creativity, if it means challenging one's superior or going outside the lines of general policy, is not. Loyalty means obedience. Formal representatives of the government do not speak for themselves; they speak for the government and they follow the official line. If they find their personal opinions or values continually or deeply at odds with official policy, they leave their jobs.

The system has two internal components that are often at odds with each other: the career employees and the political appointees, each with different cultures. Although there is frequently distrust and distance between them, good working relationships do occur. But because it is a bureaucratic system that works, as most such systems do, on the basis of personal contacts and influence, internal subgrouping or cliquishness is a common phenomenon. Some subgroups are always "in," and others are "out."

Because of the bureaucratic nature of the system, many of those who make and apply foreign policy are concerned about their own careers, and these concerns influence their behavior in numerous ways. At the same time, this field is about public service, and many of the people in it have truly unselfish motivations and seek the highest good for their nation and for the world.

The U.S. diplomatic and foreign policy community is overwhelmingly white, Eurocentric, and male. The UN system has more of a mix of people of color but is still predominantly male. This being a male-oriented world, it is infused with traditionally "masculine" values and behaviors—rationality, logic, stoicism, power orientation, crisis management, competition, aggressiveness, adversarial thinking—and with "male" language, replete, in some cases, with locker-room talk and sports analogies. In this respect it is unbalanced, lacking the more traditionally "feminine" attributes of intuition, emotion, receptivity, compassion, cooperation, and an orientation toward conciliation and relationship building over time.

Activities

The activities of the U.S. diplomatic process involve making and implementing foreign policy. Policymaking is both top down and bottom up. In the top-down process, the president and his selected advisers make decisions, often but not always after consultation with others from the State Department, the National Security Council, the Joint Chiefs of Staff, the Defense Department, Congress, the CIA, and others. In the Bush administration, for instance, the president demonstrated a highly visible and personal style of involvement in policymaking and diplomatic relations with other heads of state.

From the ground up, the State Department's worldwide network of consular and embassy staffs, through thousands of daily telegrams and reports, provide a lot of the basic information, judgment calls, and recommendations that trigger foreign policy decisions to act or not to act on a given issue. Domestically, members of the Policy Planning Staff in the State Department may meet with journalists, diplomats, human rights groups, religious groups, academics, think tanks, private citizens, and advocacy groups that wish to share information or influence policy. Feedback from these meetings is brought to interagency and interdepartmental meetings, at which recommendations are formulated to be passed on to the secretary of state.

The consultation process that happens at the State Department is repeated at the next level, with different agencies presenting their views to the National Security Council. Here too, opposing views can be aired (though the degree of openness may change from administration to administration), and some kind of consensus emerges. The president makes the final decision. Much of this process is oriented toward immediate situations; little time and few resources go to long-term planning.

Congress, too, is a player in the policymaking community, although its role vis-à-vis the executive branch is a subject of ongoing debate and ambiguity. Congressional committees hold hearings and engage in discussions with administration officials to craft legislation, and Congressional staffs conduct field visits and respond to letters and calls from lobbyists and constituents. Congress engages in a constant dance of checks and balances between the public and the administration to delineate and finance the foreign policy of the country.

Formal negotiations between representatives of nations take several forms. There are negotiations over broad agreements, specific treaties, and plans of cooperative action. There are large, international, multilateral conferences involving huge U.S. teams that consider issues affecting many nations; there are small, private negotiations between high-ranking individuals on issues of more narrow interest to two parties. There are ongoing negotiations on specific issues, formal peace negotiations to end wars, and informal peace processes extending over time.

In all these, the activity of building personal trust is critical. Because the international diplomatic community is relatively small, the same people appear over and over, perhaps with greater levels of power as time goes on. Once trusting relationships are established, they become significant links in an ongoing network of key figures as the world's drama unfolds over time.

What about the role of the United Nations in the diplomatic world? It is through the UN and its related international nongovernmental organizations that much of our international diplomacy takes place. In addition to significant peacebuilding activities in the areas of economic and social development, human rights, decolonization, and international law, the UN has both peacemaking and peacekeeping functions. Through international conferences, the good offices of the secretary-general, Security Council resolutions, peacekeeping forces, and election monitoring, the UN can have a profound impact on global peace and security issues.

The UN in the 1990s is reexamining its role in the changing landscape of peacekeeping missions, such as in Somalia and Bosnia. It is exploring areas of preventive diplomacy as well as rapid-response action forces and is improving its ability to function with round-the-clock coverage through its Operations Center. The UN is now recognizing the need for training in the field of conflict resolution and is supporting the training of its own staff through the United Nations Institute for Training and Research (UNITAR) and through the training of UN civilian peacekeepers at the Austrian Peace Institute.

Issues in the Field

Infighting, or internalized power politics, is ubiquitous throughout the U.S. governmental system. Turf battles, power struggles, and intergroup rivalry, though considered a fact of life in that world, deplete the system of resources, energy, and talent that could otherwise go to improve both the content and the process of its functioning.

Likewise, the government community's insularity from the public and its elitism, as well as the secrecy under which some of its activities occur, contribute to the mystification of Track One as a realm of unreachable experts. In fact, much relevant expertise about international relations, peace, and conflict resolution resides outside the Track One community, but the boundaries are so tight and so closely guarded that such expertise frequently has no way of getting through to the people who need access to it. This constitutes one of the major obstacles not just to the effective functioning of Track One but to the whole multi-track system. Repeated acts of political will and courage from many Track One figures will be needed to correct the situation.

Another challenge facing Track One is the need to address the role and value of peacemaking as a tool for international relations.

The lead-up to the Persian Gulf War demonstrated that the process of negotiation and communication is equated with weakness by some government leaders. The extent to which nonviolent peacemaking and conflict resolution can be legitimated by the decision makers (by themselves or under pressure from the public) may significantly determine the shape of future world events.

Finally, diplomats need increased and improved training in negotiation skills, particularly in multilateral negotiations. At present, most formal negotiators are operating without theoretical or practical training, other than their own experience and intuition. As negotiations in an interdependent, multipolar world become increasingly complex, scientific, ecological, and economic data will become crucial resources in the solving of international problems. Discussions will involve not only sovereign states but formal and informal citizens' groups, special-interest groups, and scientific and identity groups as well. Training and preparation for this development are critical.

Finally, a brief word about the key issues regarding the United Nations and its changing role in world polity: As regional and internal conflicts between identity groups become more prominent in their own right and no longer serve as proxies for East-West power struggles, the UN has an opportunity to assume a much larger role in peacemaking as the primary international authority on peace. At the same time, events in Somalia, Cambodia, Bosnia, and elsewhere have clearly shown the limitations of the UN and other international bodies. The genocide in Rwanda and the ongoing violence in the former Yugoslavia have left the entire international community wondering about the extent of its ability to prevent war and make peace in the face of determined war makers.

To address these issues, the UN will have to find creative ways of dealing with the constraints placed on it in its charter, which bars intervention in the internal affairs of sovereign nations. Since more than 90 percent of all armed conflicts are between identity groups within and across nation-state boundaries, the UN is effectively shut out from any major role in their prevention or resolution. The situations with the Kurds in Turkey and the Chechens in Russia have demonstrated to the world community the necessity of finding some way to address the needs of peoples who are unrepresented in world bodies of government.

Whether the world chooses to reassert its commitment to the original goals and intentions of the United Nations as a preeminent peacemaking body remains to be seen. Are nations willing to cede some of their jealously guarded authority and sovereignty to some larger order of political organization? This is not a rhetorical question, nor a matter of mere politics. It strikes at the very existential core of our reality, as individuals, as communities, and as nations. When one system becomes aware of the greater system of which it is a part it always faces issues of autonomy and must find a way to tolerate certain ambiguities with as much grace as possible.

In this regard, the United States might look to its closest allies, the nations of the European Union, which are struggling with these issues nation by nation. They have found that collectively they are far more powerful economically than they were as individual nation-states. The European Union is moving toward a more unitary political system, which will require member nations to give up even more national sovereignty. The changing face of other international alliances (the Organization of Security and Cooperation in Europe and the North Atlantic Treaty Organization, for instance) and the rise of geo-economics and its emerging international structures (the General Agreement on Tariffs and Trade and the World Trade Organization, for example) require Track One in the United States to examine its basic assumptions about collective security and determine how it will cope with the challenges of the next century. Profound differences of opinion on these matters between the Democratic and Republican Parties add to the complexity of this discussion.

The strength of both the United States' and the United Nations' diplomatic systems is that they provide an extensive pool of dedicated public servants with vast collective experience and expertise in solving problems and promoting peace. Although it is not always successful in employing that expertise for desired peaceful ends, Track One has the necessary resources within itself and at its disposal to generate collective, humane, effective, and creative paths for peace. Whether it has the political will for such a step remains to be seen.

Place in the Field

Track One serves as the command function of the system. It sets the agenda, and all the other components react to support, challenge, question, oppose, or seek to influence it. Track One provides the leadership or authority for the system, not internally in the life of the system but externally in its dealings with the world. By being the only official channel for international agreements, it is in charge, but like all leaders, it is open to counterdependent, or critical, response from the rest of the system, regardless of what steps it takes.

The negative potential of Track One is its rigidity, exclusivity, elitism, and potential for the abuse of power. Its institutions and thinking are strongly embedded in the state-centric mode of power politics, and it resists change.

The positive potential is its ability to mobilize vast resources to enact whatever policies it chooses. Another strength of the system is the realization of its responsibility to guide the United States and the world toward a new global order—one based on freedom, justice, and democracy. The United States, though not always embodying those principles fully in its own internal life, stands, like the Statue of Liberty, as a beacon to the rest of the world, lighting the way to hope and a better future for all. Accepting this role with the humility and compassion of one who serves the larger whole contains untold possibility for great good.

Resources

American Academy of Diplomacy
1726 M St., NW
Suite 800
Washington, DC 20036
(202) 223-0510
AAD fosters high standards for the conduct of diplomacy and foreign affairs of the United States.

Brian Atwood
U.S. Agency for International Development
2201 C St., NW
Room 5942
Washington, DC 20520
(202) 647-4330
USAID establishes the conditions for democracy and free enterprise in partner countries in the developing world through technical assistance and provides humanitarian relief in situations of natural or

man-made disasters in a manner that advances long-term development goals. USAID's efforts are designed to move nations to self-sufficiency in order to promote stability and create markets for U.S. goods, thereby advancing U.S. national security interests and the U.S. economic and trade position.

Chester A. Crocker
School of Foreign Service
Georgetown University
1316 Thirty-sixth St., NW
Washington, DC 20057
(202) 687-5074
As assistant secretary of state for African affairs during the Reagan administration, Crocker managed the eight-year peace process for Namibia.

Joseph Findlay
Department of Public Information
S 1005 United Nations
New York, NY 10017
(212) 963-6840
Findlay designs and disseminates information to the public on UN peacekeeping and election observation programs.

Vince San Fuentes
Foreign Relations Aide
Office of Senator Paul Sarbanes (D-Md.)
U.S. Senate
Washington, DC 20510
(202) 224-4524
San Fuentes interfaces with lobbyists, advocacy groups, and constituents on foreign relations issues. Advises the senator, who, as a ranking member of the Senate Foreign Relations Committee, considers legislation on all major foreign policy issues.

Barry F. Gidley
Principal Public Information Specialist
Organization of American States
1889 F St., NW
Washington, DC 20006
(202) 458-3000

The OAS secures peace in the Americas and promotes democracy and development through technical assistance.

Institute for the Study of Diplomacy
School of Foreign Service
Georgetown University
1316 Thirty-sixth St., NW
Washington, DC 20057
(202) 965-5735
Disseminates knowledge of the diplomatic process and its pivotal role in international peacemaking through studies and publications.

Aaron Miller
Deputy Special Middle East Coordinator
Office of Special Middle East Coordinator
Department of State, Room 7527
Washington, DC 20520
(202) 647- 2946
Formerly responsible for the Arab-Israeli section of the Policy Planning Staff at the State Department, Miller now works with the president's special Middle East coordinator; interfaces with journalists, academics, human rights groups, and other private citizens with an interest in the area; and works with the Bureau of Near Eastern Affairs and in interagency meetings to craft policy recommendations for the secretary of state.

Robert Müller
The University for Peace
Box 199
Escozu, Costa Rica
Former assistant secretary-general of the United Nations and chancellor of the University for Peace, Müller received the 1989 UNESCO Peace Education Prize. He is an inspiring writer and philosopher on international peace issues.

Robert W. Russell
International Monetary Fund
R. 12-510
700 Nineteenth St., NW
Washington, DC 20431
T: (202) 623-7300   F: (202) 623-6278

The IMF is an organization of 179 member nations that pledges to cooperate to facilitate the growth of international trade, raise income and employment levels, and develop the productive resources of its members.

United Nations
United Nations Secretariat
New York, NY 10017
(212) 963-1234
The United Nations is an intergovernmental organization made up of nation-states that accept the obligations of the United Nations Charter. The purposes of the United Nations are, among others, to maintain peace and international security and to cooperate internationally in solving international economic, social, cultural, and humanitarian problems.

Track Two: Nongovernment/Professional
Peacemaking through Professional
Conflict Resolution

Track Two encompasses a number of activities involving unofficial, nongovernmental citizen interactions between parties to a conflict, often but not always with the presence and assistance of a third party. The ultimate aim of these activities is to help resolve conflict by encouraging communication, understanding, and collaboration toward shared problem solving.

Track Two work is based on the assumption that unofficial discussions provide a latitude that is not available in formal settings. This freedom, in turn, offers the opportunity to examine the root causes of and the underlying human needs in conflicts, to explore possible solutions out of public view, to identify obstacles to better relationships, and to look ahead at issues not yet on the official agenda. By allowing face-to-face communication, it also helps participants arrest the dehumanization process, overcome psychological barriers, focus on relationship building, and reframe the conflict as a shared problem that can be resolved collaboratively.

Track Two is transformational, positing a worldview in which power politics is superseded by mutual empowerment; identity groups at least join if not replace nation-states as the loci of power; basic human needs and not strategic interests set the agenda; collaboration and inclusivity replace competition and exclusivity; international relations are seen as ongoing relationships between all the people, not crisis or situational relationships between governments; and the international community is called to address human and environmental issues, not just the political side of world affairs.

Shape of the Field

Unlike in Track One, where all the players are part of a single, formal, bureaucratic political system, in Track Two the actors come from many settings and do their work individually rather than through their formal affiliations. Although most of the key people in the field are employed by academic, research, or action-oriented institutions and derive professional credibility and salary through those associations, several work independently, without major affiliation or compensation.

Many of the key spokespeople for the field originally came out of the Track One or governmental system; others came from religious, psychological, labor, or legal backgrounds. Several have experience with social movements, community action programs, or educational administration. The disciplines involved tend to be in the social and political fields: political science, government, international relations, law, sociology, social psychology, peace studies, and behavioral science.

Some people engaged in this work are primarily theoreticians or practitioners; most, however, are a mixture of both. Among the theoreticians are those who address the specifics of Track Two activities (problem-solving workshops, mediation modalities) and those who address a wider conceptualization of the work in its sundry contexts (the role of psychology in understanding conflict, the change from power politics to mutual empowerment, the need for Track Two to relate to Track One). Among the practitioners, some work from a particular conceptual model, whereas others are more freewheeling, doing what feels right in the situation and trusting their experience and intuition. Some are technique oriented, believing that a particular methodology is the right intervention; others are relationship oriented, believing that various methods might be employed to enhance a more positive relationship between conflicting parties.

Culture

Track Two is primarily a professional system; the participants are predominantly male and almost exclusively white and range in age from forty to eighty. It has a strong intellectual, academic bias, and most of its key players have either Ph.D. or J.D. degrees. This means that academic and professional credibility—and the personal bearing, behavior, and norms that are commonly associated with it—is highly valued in the system.

However, the work also has a strong social value base—at times, a radical one. For most people in the field, the work is seen as transformational. By emphasizing the human, humane, nonviolent, relational, interactive, shared, mutually empowered aspects of resolving conflicts and building relationships, Track Two is the leading edge of the whole Multi-Track Diplomacy system, based on the realities of the interdependent, multipolar, transnational, identity group–focused world that is our planetary context for the twenty-first century.

Track Two work is generally not compatible with a comfortable nine-to-five kind of life. It involves long hours, frequent travel, and intense interactions. It often takes practitioners from their pleasant middle-class lives and drops them into the suffering and anguish of war-torn settings or brings those affected by war into their homes and offices. This requires dedication, a service commitment, and a profound sense of compassion.

The field is growing and changing rapidly, with women and younger generations of theoreticians and practitioners bringing attention to new issues, including the need for the Track Two community to be more consonant within its own system and with the values and methodologies it espouses for others.

Activities

The activities of Track Two diplomacy are varied. They include problem-solving workshops, involvement as mediators or consultants to ongoing peacemaking processes, private one-on-one diplomacy, conferences, seminars, training and education events, dialogue groups, networking, confidence building, institution building, and acting as messengers or go-betweens. In addition to the practice of conflict resolution, there is the whole realm of conceptualizing about it, which includes analyzing events and developing theoretical frameworks that are descriptive and predictive. There is also some activity that looks at the field as a field and helps it define and evaluate itself.

Issues in the Field

We can distinguish here between those issues that relate to the content of conflict resolution work and those that address the development of the Track Two field itself.

In terms of the content, certain major questions dominate the field. One concerns the possibility of managing conflict resolution processes more consciously and systemically: can the many individuals from different tracks involved in simultaneous and overlapping efforts at conflict resolution be organized and coordinated for a more effective outcome? In a similar vein, can conflicts best be resolved from the ground up, with the help of mediators who are insiders in the system, or should there be an intervention from outside experts? What is the legitimate relationship or mix between the two? Are there indigenous modes of conflict resolution within the cultures of the parties that could be called forth and utilized? If so, how and by whom? How culturally appropriate are our Western conflict resolution technologies in other settings?

Is the role of the facilitator to manage a process that is ultimately about relationship building or to achieve a specific outcome? Is there a legitimate place for the third party's personal perceptions, judgments, and emotions in the process, or must he or she stay as objective as possible?

Regarding conflicts in which the power disparities between the parties are great and one side is clearly treating the other unjustly, how does the facilitator help establish parity or use the power imbalance to open channels for creative thinking? How can we ripen a conflict or change the political context so that the parties will want to seek resolution? After a problem-solving workshop, training session, conference, or other such event, how do we help people reenter their original systems and transfer the learning appropriately?

Finally, a major challenge of this work concerns dealing with deeply embedded group psychological issues: victimhood, mourning, forgiveness, and contrition. How do we engage a whole identity group, or at least its leaders and key figures, in working toward the kind of ritual and substantive psychological change that needs to happen for true reconciliation, for true peace to take hold? What happens to the children, the refugees, the wounded after the guns go silent?

In terms of the development of the field itself, one of the critical issues is language. Certain key phrases such as *conflict resolution, peace-making, prenegotiation, win-win, win-lose, conflict settlement, conflict management,* and *conflict transformation* have different connotations for different people. Should these phrases be standardized in meaning, and if so, by whom?

Another challenge relates to identity group differences within the field itself. How does the field make space for women, people of color, other cultures, and new generations of practitioners in ways that genuinely incorporate their unique wisdom? Most of the conflict resolution work done in the field takes place in Third World countries and involves identity group issues. It is the elders who are invited to intervene, so they control the opportunities for the younger generation to receive the direct experience needed to develop as practitioners. It therefore behooves the field to do its own diversity modeling.

Probably the biggest single challenge facing the field is money. The funding community is accustomed to looking for product, but conflict resolution is a process. Foundations want time-limited projects with clear objectives and measurable outcomes, but conflict resolution is an open-ended process with impossible-to-measure results. Adding to these difficulties are the financial constraints of the work itself. There are often great travel expenses involved, and a long-term though perhaps sporadic time commitment is required. Sometimes the call to work is immediate. Raising money within these parameters is extraordinarily difficult and requires an entirely different set of skills than the conflict resolution work.

This is intimately related to the need to enhance the credibility of the field, which may require some institutionalization. Many Track Two experts believe that there needs to be a better definition of the field and an infrastructure from which to build a means of educating the public, sponsoring institutions, funders, and policymakers about the value of conflict resolution as a mature and legitimate discipline.

As the field professionalizes, it must also deal with ethical issues. Intervening in conflicts carries innate moral concerns about power, sensitivity, authority, ethnocentricity, personal agenda, and commitment, among others. Facilitation may actually harm rather than help the process.

Finally, the field must find a way to educate those from whom it seeks legitimacy. The creative use of media, lobbying techniques, and demonstration projects offers opportunities to help policymakers and the public know and value the work of conflict resolution. Ultimately, the work of Track Two must be fed into and work cooperatively with that of Track One. Neither of the tracks can operate effectively without the other, but finding those avenues of communication and cooperation is proving to be a long and difficult process. This is especially so given the traditional elitism of Track One, and given that the premises of Track Two are distinct from the Track One assumptions about power relations.

The strength of Track Two is that it is a field whose time has come. Students are flooding into college and university programs to learn about peace, conflict resolution, and peacemaking. War and violence as solutions for local and global problems are becoming increasingly horrifying and endlessly repetitive. New ways are desperately needed, and Track Two has the theory base, the practical methodologies, and the committed personnel to address this need.

Place in the Field

Track Two plays a self-regulating role in the Multi-Track Diplomacy system. It recognizes that the structures of Track One are not sufficient to address all the needs of peacemaking and creates and produces complementary procedures to fill the gaps. It is the leading edge of the system, reaching into new territory and bringing the rest of the system with it to explore new possibilities.

The negative aspect of Track Two is that, in being the regulating mechanism of the whole system, it runs the risk of being unregulated itself or being widely dispersed, not grounded in itself or within the system. The positive side is that it is naming and addressing the issues facing the system with great clarity and creativity. It is playing a transformational role by positing a process that takes us beyond power politics and allows us to seek concrete ways for all peoples to become meaningful members of the family of humanity. By taking us to the very edge of our knowledge about the psychological processes of large-group human behavior, Track Two is extending the peacemaking mode far beyond conflict resolution to the uncharted territory of planetary healing.

Resources

Landrum Bolling
Conflict Management Group
20 University Rd.
Cambridge, MA 02138
(617) 354-5444
Scott Brown, executive director
A longtime behind-the-scenes Track Two practitioner, Bolling has
worked extensively to facilitate communication and human rights
intervention in the Middle East and with the former Soviet Union
and Eastern Europe. He is on the advisory committee for the Institute for Multi-Track Diplomacy.

John Burton
13 Jaeger Circuit, Bruce
ACT. 2617
Australia
F: 61-625-17840
Burton originated the needs-based, problem-solving workshop
approach to conflict resolution and started six conflict resolution
centers around the world. He is a respected elder in the conflict
resolution world.

Jimmy Carter
Conflict Resolution Program
International Negotiation Network
The Carter Center of Emory University
One Copenhill
Atlanta, GA 30307
T: (404) 420-5151   F: (404) 420-5196
Harry Barnes, director
This program was developed by former President Jimmy Carter in
1987 to provide a network of individuals who can serve as inter-
national mediators and conflict resolution consultants. Carter is
frequently called on for election monitoring, mediation, and behind-
the-scenes talks with disputing parties. Because of his prominence
as a former president, Carter is able to serve as a bridge between
Track One and Track Two diplomacy.

CDR Associates
100 Arapahoe Ave.
Suite 12
Boulder, CO 80302
(303) 442-7367
Contact: Peter Woodrow
CDR (Communication/Decisions/Results) provides conflict management assistance to businesses, governmental agencies, professionals, and organizations in the public sector. CDR has a staff of professional mediators and facilitators who contract with individuals and organizations to assist them in resolving their conflicts in an amicable and cost-effective manner. CDR is also known nationally and internationally for its training programs in decision making, team building, negotiation, facilitation, and mediation.

Center for International Understanding
230 S. Bemiston
Suite 411
St. Louis, MO 63105
T/F: (314) 721-8580
Carol Cook, executive director
CIU is engaged in creating a worldwide network of diplomats skilled in fostering international cooperation and reducing violent conflict. Its work focuses on the creation of weeklong multilateral educational conferences and other activities designed to develop skills in conflict prevention and resolution, reduce prejudice, and build constructive problem-solving relationships within the network.

Kevin P. Clements
Institute of Conflict Analysis and Resolution
George Mason University
4400 University Dr., Mail Stop 4D3
Fairfax, VA 22030-4444
T: (703) 993-1300   F: (703) 993-1302
Clements is the president of the International Peace Research Association. As an educator with an interest in UN reform, his Track Two regional focus is Asia Pacific, with an emphasis on preventive diplomacy and building peace and international community.

Conflict Management Group
20 University Rd.

Cambridge, MA 02138
T: (617) 354-5444   F: (617) 354-8467
Contact: Diana Chigas
Conflict Management Group is dedicated to improving the methods
of negotiation, conflict resolution, and cooperative decision making
as applied to issues of public concern. It is engaged in training
negotiators, consulting, diagnostic research, conflict analysis, facilitation, consensus building, and mediation.

Tom Colosi, Vice President
Office of National Affairs
American Arbitration Association
1150 Connecticut Ave., NW
Suite 605
Washington, DC 20036
T: (202) 331-7073   F: (202) 331-3356
Colosi has extensive experience as an advocate, trainer, and third
party in bilateral and multilateral negotiations and other dispute
settlement processes. He is the author of numerous articles and
books on training techniques and negotiation and is a board mem-
ber of the Institute for Multi-Track Diplomacy.

Conflict Resolution Catalysts
PO Box 836
Montpelier, VT 05601
T/F: (802) 229-1165
Contact: Gary Shapiro
This group's mission is to develop, promote, and coordinate citizen-
based peacemaking and conflict resolution, with its main project
in Bosnia-Herzegovina.

Louise Diamond
Institute for Multi-Track Diplomacy
1819 H St., NW
Suite 1200
Washington, DC 20006
T: (202) 466-4605   F: (202) 466-4607
Diamond works to promote the transformation of deep-rooted con-
flict through training, dialogue, and education projects. She is involved
in programs in Cyprus, the Middle East, the Horn of Africa, and East
Asia.

Roger Fisher
Harvard Law School
Cambridge, MA 02138
(617) 495-4615
Fisher has been a third-party facilitator to innumerable international
negotiations. He is a champion of the "win-win" approach to
negotiation as shared problem solving and is a renowned teacher,
author, and consultant in the field.

Ron Fisher
Department of Psychology
University of Saskatchewan
Saskatoon, Saskatchewan
S7N 0W0 Canada
T: (306) 966-6818   F: (306) 966-6630
Professor of social psychology and a scholar practitioner in the field
of conflict resolution, Fisher is also an author, trainer, and researcher.
He has focused recently on the island of Cyprus.

Foundation for a Global Community
222 High St.
Palo Alto, CA 94301-1097
T: (415) 328-7756   F: (415) 328-7785
Contact: Eileen Rinde
The foundation's mission is to discover, live, and communicate what
is needed to build a world that functions for the benefit of all life,
with a continuing focus on violence between peoples.

Paula Gutlove
The Balkan Peace Project
27 Ellsworth Ave.
Cambridge, MA 02139
(617) 491-5177
Gutlove works with the Track Two community to advance the field
of interactive conflict resolution. She is the director of a project to
bring conflict resolution training to key parties in the Balkans.

IDR Associates
1901 Pennsylvania Ave., NW
Suite 500
Washington, DC 20006

T: (202) 466-5120   F: (202) 466-5669
Contact: Alissa J. Stern
IDR (International Dispute Resolution) Associates provides training, systems design, and intervention in international dispute resolution and prevention.

Herbert C. Kelman
Richard Clarke Cabot Professor of Social Ethics
Director, Program on International Conflict Analysis
    and Resolution
Harvard University
William James Hall 1430
Cambridge, MA 02138
T: (617) 495-3816   F: (617) 495-3728
Kelman is a major figure in developing the field of interactive problem solving through teaching, writing, and facilitating problem-solving workshops. He has been involved in more than forty such workshops, most concerning the Palestinian-Israeli conflict.

Louis Kriesberg
Program on the Analysis and Resolution of Conflict
Maxwell School of Citizenship and Public Affairs
Syracuse University
410 Maxwell Hall
Syracuse, NY 13244-4400
(315) 443-2367
Kriesberg is a major contributor to the development of the theory and practice of transforming intractable conflicts.

John Paul Lederach
International Conciliation Service of the Mennonite Central
    Committee and Conflict Analysis and Transformation Program
Institute for Conflict Studies and Peace Building
Eastern Mennonite University
Harrisonburg, VA 22801-2462
T: (540) 432-4490   F: (540) 432-4449 or 4444
Lederach is a key figure in the theory and practice of the elicitive model of conflict resolution. He has worked extensively in Central America and with the Basques and within the Mennonite community doing predictive and preventive work. His focus is on empowering indigenous peacemaking.

Bill Lincoln
National Center Association Inc.
3924 N. Thirty-second St.
Tacoma, WA 98407
T: (206) 567-4307   F: (206) 597-8103
Lincoln started his career as a labor management arbitrator three decades ago and moved into the field of international conflict resolution training, with a special focus on the environment. He has worked in more than a dozen countries around the world.

John Marks
Search for Common Ground
1601 Connecticut Ave., NW
Suite 200
Washington, DC 20009
T: (202) 265-4300   F: (202) 232-6718
This group advances the use of innovative, nonadversarial methods of resolving international and domestic policy disputes and promotes action based on what unites individuals, groups, and nations—not what separates them. It has concentrated on the Middle East, South Africa, Macedonia, Burundi, and the Network for Life and Choice (dialogue between pro-life [anti-abortion] and pro-choice communities).

Susan Collins Marks
1851 Mintwood Pl., NW
Washington, DC 20009
T/F: (202) 387-8277
Marks has expertise in political and community conflict resolution and in police-community relations. Under the auspices of South Africa's National Peace Accord, she served on the Western Cape Peace Committee Executive. She also edited a quarterly publication entitled *Track Two*. She was a Jennings Randolph Peace Fellow at the U.S. Institute of Peace in 1994–95.

John W. McDonald
Institute for Multi-Track Diplomacy
1819 H St., NW
Suite 1200
Washington, DC 20006
T: (202) 466-4605   F: (202) 466-4607

Building on a forty-year diplomatic career with the State Department, McDonald is a leading expert on multilateral negotiations and Track Two diplomacy. He is also an author, lecturer, trainer, and consultant in conflict resolution.

Christopher Mitchell
Institute of Conflict Analysis and Resolution
George Mason University
4400 University Dr., Mail Stop 4D3
Fairfax, VA 22030-4444
T: (703) 993-1300   F: (703) 993-1302
Mitchell works with the problem-solving approach as a means of effecting change and as a research tool. He is an experienced facilitator, teacher, and researcher in conflict resolution.

Joseph V. Montville
Center for Strategic and International Studies
1800 K St., NW
Suite 400
Washington, DC 20006
T: (202) 775-3277   F: (202) 775-3199
Involved in research, writing, and theory building in Track Two diplomacy, Montville is instrumental in fostering awareness of the role of psychological issues in the conflict resolution process. He is a member of the advisory council of the Institute for Multi-Track Diplomacy.

Partners for Democratic Change
823 Ulloa St.
San Francisco, CA 94127
(415) 665-0652
Raymond Shonholtz, president
PDC seeks to advance a culture of conflict resolution in the developing new democracies. It has set up conflict resolution centers throughout Eastern Europe and Russia.

Program on International Conflict Analysis and Resolution
Center for International Affairs
Harvard University
1737 Cambridge St.
Cambridge, MA 02138

T: (617) 496-0680   F: (617) 496-7370
Contact: Donna Hicks
PICAR is devoted to advancing the understanding of international
and interethnic conflicts and to developing interactive problem-
solving processes that can be effective in managing or resolving such
conflicts.

Jay Rothman
Haverford College
Haverford, PA 19041
T: (610) 896-1062   F: (610) 896-1495
Rothman is active in developing the theory, training, and practice
of prenegotiation models. He works specifically with the Arab-Israeli
conflict.

Abdul Aziz Said
Director, Peace and Conflict Resolution Studies
The American University
4400 Massachusetts Ave., NW
Washington, DC 20016-8071
T: (202) 885-1632 or 1622   F: (202) 885-6999
Said is active in behind-the-scenes communications and confidence
building, particularly between the United States and the Arab world
and in ecumenical meetings of Jews, Christians, and Muslims.

Harold Saunders
Director, International Affairs
Kettering Foundation
444 North Capital St., NW
Suite 434
Washington, DC 20001-1512
T: (202) 393-4478   F: (202) 393-7644
Saunders is retired from high-level positions in the Department of
State, where he participated in the mediation of five Arab-Israeli
agreements, including the Camp David Accords and the Egyptian-
Israeli Peace Treaty, at the height of the peace process, 1973–78.
He is now a preeminent writer and thinker on Track One–Track
Two diplomacy, focusing on conflict resolution and the strength-
ening of civil society. At the Kettering Foundation, Saunders runs a
dialogue process with parties to the civil war in Tajikistan.

Vamik D. Volkan
Center for the Study of Mind and Human Interaction
Blue Ridge Hospital, Drawer A
Charlottesville, VA 22901
T: (804) 924-9001   F: (804) 924-2439
As a psychiatrist, Volkan has been instrumental in elucidating the psychodynamics of international relationships and is an eminent writer on the subject.

Dudley Weeks
Global Future Links
2400 Forty-first St., NW, #100
Washington, DC 20007
T/F: (202) 337-7574
Weeks is an independent practitioner, teacher, and trainer in conflict resolution, with extensive experience in South Africa.

Track Three: Business
Peacemaking through Commerce

The primary task of business in the peace and conflict resolution process, beyond making a profit, is to build relationships and create pathways for communication and joint action. It also serves to enhance the economic health of peoples and nations, thereby relieving some of the economic pressures of poverty and need that can lead to conflict. Finally, trade is a major vehicle through which our global interdependence is actualized, so it can be a doorway to bonds of mutual trust and benefit that strengthen the whole global family.

A major assumption on which the relationship between business and peace rests is that international business can be a positive, mutually beneficial proposition for all the parties. Another is that business is not an isolated phenomenon but an integral part of the social and political fabric of international life. A third is that business, when conducted with social and environmental consciousness, can be a major force for positive change in large transnational systems and in government thinking. Finally, most businesses recognize that there can be no successful business without peace.

Shape of the Field

The international business community actively engaged in peacebuilding activities includes a wide spectrum of organizations. They range from multinational corporations that are deeply embedded in the economic structure of many countries to individual entrepreneurs or small companies that have some rudimentary contacts and financial dealings outside the United States. Also in this field, for purposes of this book, are business associations whose activities support some kind of peace work and those schools or educational programs that teach business diplomacy or pursue the possibilities of using trade as a tool of international political policy.

Culture

The business world represented in this book comprises two very different subcultures. The mainstream business community is traditionally conservative, profit oriented, and competitive. There is also a growing group of socially conscious businesses that come from a more progressive culture, which could be described as more liberal, environmentally conscious, peace and justice oriented, and cooperative. At present, both communities are represented primarily by white males.

Activities

This track is probably the least well developed and defined of the nine tracks. Most businesses do not see themselves as having anything to do with peace. Even those multinational corporations that have long seen the cross-cultural benefits of their endeavors might hesitate to acknowledge their role as peacemakers. They might, however, acknowledge a peacebuilding role through the creation of strong bonds of relationship, understanding, and communication between peoples of different nations.

This peacebuilding function is important. International business, by definition, brings together nationals from different countries, and they must learn to work together. This requires some cracking of our natural ethnocentric lens and an opening up to new cultures, new perspectives, new friendships. These friendships can go very deep and spread through extended family structures to give many people a sense of community and relatedness. American businesses, especially those operating in developing nations, have many resources to offer. They can provide opportunities for schooling, health care, career training and development, and other related services that are often received with profound gratitude by recipients, winning lifelong friendships. By involving themselves in local community projects and events, businesses also strengthen interpersonal bonds.

The opportunity for travel provided by international business is the original citizen exchange program, bringing people to new settings where they can learn about one another's lives and dreams. When a complex network of such cross-cultural friendships exists, government policy cannot help but be affected.

When a U.S. company has major business investments in another country, it inevitably takes note of the social, economic, and political conditions in that setting. To improve its business success, it will naturally want to do what it can to protect its investment. This can mean anything from improving the living conditions of its workers to seeking to influence U.S. foreign and trade policies. Likewise, a citizenry that has traveled the world and worked abroad will have a sense of relationship with the countries and cultures it has visited and will be more informed and attentive to policy issues concerning those places.

Business can play an active role in peacemaking as well. Having developed networks of contacts throughout various levels of the host country's government, U.S. businesses on foreign soil can use those contacts to carry messages to heads of state directly or, more indirectly, to convey ideas and suggestions informally between parties. They can also be called upon to provide their good offices in local disputes. Businesses that have been ensconced in a location for a long time will have a wide and deep knowledge about that country and could be useful consultants to the process of determining foreign policy, especially in crisis situations.

A major activity in the socially conscious business community is the development of market cooperatives, whereby indigenous groups of artisans in developing nations sell their products through U.S. outlets. This segment of the business community is also involving itself with various environmental, economic, and social issues in host countries and seeking to educate Americans about the relationship between business and conscious consumerism. Overlapping some of the work of the development community, these businesses are finding ways to empower local agricultural and manufacturing workers toward self-sufficiency with environmentally sustainable methods and natural, indigenous raw materials.

In this field, too, are those associations that seek to support a particular relationship between business and peace, be it through the education of the policymaking community about business issues or the potential for greater use of government and business resources for peaceful ends. One organization, Business for Peace in Iowa (no longer active), worked to educate itself on peace and security issues and to influence local and national decision makers on key concerns.

There are also educational and action programs for those who wish to learn international business management and business diplomacy and negotiation and to help build democratic economic structures in rapidly changing political systems.

Issues in the Field

A major issue facing the business community is its responsibility for the environment, especially as U.S. businesses go into Eastern Europe and other already heavily degraded environments. The line between responsibility and profitability has been shifting over the last decade and will continue to shift as environmental needs become more compelling and environmental sustainability becomes less a fashionable trend and more a necessity for survival.

The business community is challenged to attend to its social responsibility in Third World countries. The public is increasingly demonstrating, through boycotts and other means, that it will not tolerate the sending of materials, goods, and waste products that do not meet basic health and safety standards here to unsuspecting and unprotected peoples of the Third World. As American labor forces are abandoned for cheaper labor elsewhere, businesses must guard against the tendency to create new forms of economic colonialism.

Most of the same issues facing the political world—diversity and identity group needs, collective cooperation versus individual competition, creative and shared problem solving, building new forms in rapidly changing systems—are also important to the business community in its role as a peaceful link between peoples. Track Three, like the rest of the Multi-Track Diplomacy system, is called to address its internal processes as well as external activities to come into alignment around these issues. It will have to be more inclusive of women and people of color, explore the depolarization of relations among its own internal factions, and confront the relationship between its moral responsibility for a healthy planet and its bottom-line concerns.

The defense and arms industries will be greatly challenged, both ethically and financially, in the coming years to join the trend away from violence as a tool for problem solving. Economic conversion of defense manufacturing to goods that are more sustaining of life is beginning to be a significant trend in the business world and will need to become more so.

One of the most open-ended challenges for business is to help economic systems develop and emerge after the breakdown of communism in Eastern Europe and Central Asia. Likewise, the economic development of strife-torn areas such as the Gaza Strip or South Africa can mean the difference between continued violence or true peacebuilding. These challenges will require the business community to confront all its assumptions and procedures. It must create new hybrid forms and truly innovative methods of achieving economic partnership and health where the foundations for market economies are not embedded in the fabric of society, as they are here. Patience, flexibility, risk taking, and creativity will be essential to this long-term process.

International business and trade matters are fast joining geopolitical concerns as the critical factors in international relationships. Geo-economics, as this trend is being called, is increasingly the focus of disputes, alliances, and posturing between nations, as in the U.S.-Japan trade disputes or the perennial question of most favored nation status for China in congressional deliberations. American and transnational business have deeply vested interests in these concerns and become, to some extent, both a party to emerging geo-economic disputes and a resource for their resolution.

Above all, the business community needs to increase its self-awareness and knowledge about the critical role it can play in the field of peace and conflict resolution. It has enormous resources to offer to the rest of the system. It has a massive international network in place around the globe, with useful information about economic, political, and social issues as they affect people's lives and government policies. It also has a vast, untapped financial capability to assist other activities in the Multi-Track Diplomacy system. By becoming a partner in systemic peacemaking processes, business could serve its own economic goals while serving the process of peace.

Place in the Field

Track Three is the exchange mechanism of the system. That is, it opens the doors of relationship between the private and public sectors of this and virtually all the nations of the earth and invites two-way exchange or communication. Although its medium of exchange is ostensibly goods and services, it creates pathways by which goodwill, information, friendship, and mutual respect can flow freely as well.

The negative side of business is its propensity to exploit humanity—especially the weakest segments of it—for its own gain and its tendency to operate based on greed for money and power. Its positive side is its potential for bringing disadvantaged peoples into the flow of commerce and well-being and for releasing its vast financial resources to fund the efforts of other parts of the system.

Resources

Business for Social Responsibility
1030 Fifteenth St., NW
Suite 1010
Washington, DC 20005
(202) 842-5400
Robert Dunn, president
This trade association lobbies government and businesses to work toward responsible public policy.

Center for International Private Enterprise
U.S. Chamber of Commerce
1615 H St., NW
Washington, DC 20062-2000
(202) 463-5901
John D. Sullivan, executive director
The center assists other countries through the private sector to enhance democracy and private enterprise as a basis for prosperity and individual freedom.

Coca-Cola Co.
PO Drawer 1734

Atlanta, GA 30301
(404) 676-2254
Claus M. Halle, chief international consultant
John Hunter, international director
This company uses its product (a bottle of Coke) as an international symbol of friendship; provides jobs, training, and business experience; stimulates local economies; and develops friendships all over the world. Coca-Cola works closely with governments to build frameworks for trade and investment.

Diomedes, Inc.
1278 Sacramento St.
San Francisco, CA 94108
(415) 771-8794
Jim Garrison, president
This international consulting firm is oriented toward joint business ventures between the United States and other countries.

Fourth Freedom Forum
803 North Main St.
Goshen, IN 46526
(219) 534-3402
David Cortright, president
The forum promotes the civilized defense plan—using the power of trade to prevent armed aggression—and works for the worldwide reduction of arms.

Global Business Network
PO Box 8395
Emeryville, CA 94662
T: (510) 547-6822   F: (510) 547-8510
Contact: Jim Butcher
This membership organization of individuals and corporations specializes in the use of scenarios as a tool for thinking about the future.

International Business Diplomacy Program
School of Foreign Service
Georgetown University
Washington, DC 20057
(202) 687-5854

Contact: John M. Kline
This program teaches business negotiations as they relate to government policies and deals with public policy and Third World development issues from both business and government perspectives.

Pathways to Peace
PO Box 1057
Larkspur, CA 94977
T: (415) 461-0500   F: (415) 925-0330
Contact: Avon Mattison
This is an international nonprofit Peace Messenger Organization that runs a "Peacebuilding through Business" inquiry.

Stoner Broadcasting System
410 Severn Ave.
Suite 413
Annapolis, MD 21403
(410) 263-1030
Thomas Stoner, chairman
Stoner is interested in international communications and conflict resolution and is cofounder of the Conflict Clinic.

Track Four: Private Citizen
Peacemaking through Personal Involvement

Private citizens work through many types of organizations and associations to have a direct impact on international relations. This grassroots approach seeks to establish personal relationships with people from other nations and cultures and, through those relationships, to address issues of mutual concern, break down stereotypes and promote friendship, provide needed resources, and educate the public and the policymakers on international peace and development issues. The major assumptions of such an approach are:

- Each person can make a difference.
- When the people lead, the leaders will follow.
- We are all peacemakers.
- We can take personal responsibility for changing our world.
- Power resides not just with the decision makers but at the grassroots level.
- When we have personal relationships with others, we inevitably find our common humanity and are not likely to view them as "enemies."
- People cannot be at peace when they are hungry or impoverished; peace and development are partners, and neither can exist effectively without the other.

Shape of the Field

We found five major groupings or types of nongovernmental organizations in this track: (1) citizen diplomacy or exchange programs,

(2) private voluntary organizations or development programs, (3) advocacy or special-interest groups, (4) professional interest groups, and (5) democracy-building institutions. In addition, there are some individuals working without organizational association, developing projects that they believe are appropriate, and some organizations that offer a wide range of services and programs.

Culture

This subsystem draws mostly from the middle class and attracts a large number of professional people, but its style is casual and informal. This is a value-based area, with people choosing to involve themselves because of personal ideals that emphasize sharing, cooperation, multiculturalism, service, and personal empowerment.

There is some ethnic diversity in this community, especially in the advocacy groups, where African Americans, Arab Americans, Asian Americans, Hispanic Americans, and others attempt to address the concerns of the people in their original homelands. This community also attracts women in large numbers and is one of the few in which women hold significant positions of power and influence.

Unlike most of the other tracks, citizen involvement can be avocational rather than vocational for many of its adherents. Although the staffs of some citizen organizations may be small, participants in their programs may be numerous.

Activities

Citizen diplomacy programs include both travel activities and formal dialogues or conferences on specific topics. The travel mode of citizen diplomacy has matured over the last ten years, beginning with the burgeoning of visits to and exchanges with the former Soviet Union. There are now special visits arranged to many parts of the world with any number of themes: health, business, psychology, sobriety, families, religion, politics, human rights, environment, music, art, law, women, police, education, agriculture, economics, conflict resolution, and so forth. These and similar topics have also become the subject of major conferences or dialogue programs. Although much of this activity focused on U.S.-Soviet relations to begin with, there is now increasing interest in such programs in the Middle East, Eastern Europe, and Central and South America.

This community is increasingly moving into action modes: initiating joint projects, business ventures, and communication linkups. It is also providing cross-cultural training, leadership development, scientific exchange, technical assistance, and student exchange.

As citizens return from these trips or reflect on their experiences hosting foreign visitors, they are finding creative ways to share their learning with others. They extrapolate their new awarenesses to wider issues of global education through writing, public speaking, citizen forums, and the production of school programs and curricula, action kits, videotapes, and other educational materials.

The private voluntary organizations involved in Third World development often have local grassroots support systems whereby U.S. citizens can get involved without leaving home. Fund-raisers, newsletters, dinners, concerts, and local events of all kinds keep the constituency aware, involved, and interested. The overseas work continues to empower impoverished and struggling peoples in developing nations and to provide humanitarian relief to victims of war, famine, and drought. This local grassroots constituency can be mobilized for action, which, combined with public education and advocacy work, seeks to guarantee that government policies will reflect the needs of Third World people, which are not always the same as the needs of political systems.

Advocacy groups are often single-issue organizations, focusing on one group of people or one international situation and seeking to educate the public and influence the policymakers toward specific policies. Advocacy groups often sponsor public forums, boycotts, media events, professional conferences, and, of course, regular lobbying activities.

Professional interest groups, such as Physicians for Social Responsibility, Educators for Social Responsibility, or Psychologists for Social Responsibility, are avenues for like-minded citizens to band together to pursue specific topics related to their professions. Like the other citizen groups, they tend to sponsor international delegations, conferences, joint projects, media projects, and public forums and to identify particular policies or political issues about which to educate themselves, the public, and policymakers.

Finally, there is a growing field of nongovernmental bodies dealing with democracy building in newly emerging states. These organizations provide education about democracy, election monitoring, parliamentary exchanges, and political party development and consultation on all sorts of issues related to nation building. With the humanitarian and relief agencies, these organizations are often the front line for American citizens who see and know how life is for people in places of conflict and strife. They are the knowledge holders in two directions—transferring Western wisdom in one direction and the direct experience of other people's needs in another.

Issues in the Field

One of the greatest challenges for Track Four is what to do with all the information and energy it has. With access to so much knowledge about the real-life experiences of people who are the subject of U.S. foreign policy, how do citizen peacemakers and citizen diplomats actually bring that wisdom to policymakers? How can they translate their view of the details of daily life in Rwandan refugee camps, Rumanian hospitals, Nicaraguan cooperatives, or Azeri markets, along with their profound personal caring, to the macropolitical level?

Another challenge is dealing with despair. For those whose work takes them to the developing world or to conflict zones, the seemingly unrelenting suffering of the people they meet is deeply painful. They may get enthused and energized to take personal action, yet they may also run into apathy, stonewalling, and disinterest at home.

The strength of this subsystem lies in its extensive and empowered grassroots network in the United States and all over the world. The activities of this community touch the lives of huge numbers of people, and in many cases, those people can be mobilized for various forms of action. Because of these networks, the subsystem has access to intimate knowledge of the effects of U.S. policies on the ground and on the relationship between social, economic, and political situations and peace.

U.S. citizen peacemakers and citizen diplomats abound in small-town, rural, suburban, and urban America. They span a broad range of economic and social classes, religions, and professions.

As these individuals educate themselves, they invariably find ways to educate their friends, peers, neighbors, and political leaders so that they constitute a massive and enthusiastic force for changing community and national norms, assumptions, and, ultimately, policies.

Their activities are often transformational, changing personal lives dramatically while breaking down negative images and stereotypes of others, transcending feelings of hopelessness and powerlessness, and forging strong international links and channels for ongoing communication. Although many of the individuals involved in Track Four work are invisible to the public eye, their combined activities and experience constitute a potential for peacebuilding and peacemaking whose power is just beginning to be understood.

Place in the Field

Track Four is the alternative power source of the system. It calls forth citizen power by the thousands, the millions, to open doors and improve relations at the grassroots level. It works not so much in opposition to Track One and the rest of the system as parallel with it. It provides a way for people to get involved, to be empowered to shape the global relations of a world that is, after all, not about governments but about human beings.

The negative side of Track Four is that, by being parallel with the work of Track One, it may find itself working separately from rather than hand in hand with the other components of the system. It needs to build bridges so that the citizen empowerment it engenders can both be incorporated into and lead the way for the rest of the system, especially Tracks One and Two.

The positive potential is the incredible energy released when people of different cultures and nations take their destiny into their own hands and form relationships and alliances that break down barriers to peace and harmony. Although it can never be proved, the thousands of Americans who were involved in transnational citizen peacemaking with their counterparts in the former Soviet Union have no doubt that their efforts had everything to do with the dramatic changes in U.S.-Russian relations at the end of the Cold War.

Resources

Burlington/Puerto Cabezas Sister City Program
21 Church St.
Burlington, VT 05401
(802) 865-4074
Mary Brook, director
This program links people of the two cities by providing material aid (health, education, agricultural equipment, food), work brigades (construction, gardens), educational exchanges, and school support. It is involved in projects to promote self-sufficiency and self-reliance.

Center for Citizen Initiatives
3268 Sacramento St.
San Francisco, CA 94115
T: (415) 346-1875   F: (415) 346-3731
Dale Needles, executive director
The center is a catalyst in nonofficial efforts to develop a working relationship between the states of the former Soviet Union and the United States. Programs are designed to create exchanges of information in diverse areas. The center was one of the early pioneers in the field.

Esalen Institute
Russian American Center
345 Franklin St.
San Francisco, CA 94102
(408) 667-3000
This was one of the early pioneering programs to conduct exchanges and cooperative programs with Soviet and American individuals and groups.

Robert Fuller
1716 Parker St.
Berkeley, CA 94703
T: (503) 841-0964   F: (503) 845-1628
Fuller is an independent citizen peacemaker undertaking projects in various countries that are directed at shaping public opinion and creating an atmosphere in which professional conflict resolution can operate. He writes extensively and is the founder of the Mo Tzu

project of citizen diplomacy to encourage different cultures to see their rivals as complementary parts of a larger whole. He says that he seeks "a better game than war."

InterAction
American Council for Voluntary International Action
1717 Massachusetts Ave., NW
Suite 801
Washington, DC 22036
(202) 667-8227
This coalition of over 100 private and voluntary organizations is dedicated to international humanitarian issues. It is involved in disaster relief; refugee protection, assistance, and resettlement; long-term development; public policy; and educating the American public on international development issues.

Iowa Peace Institute
917 Tenth Ave.
Grinnell, IA 50112
(515) 236-4880
Gregg Buntz, president
Organized by a group of concerned Iowa citizens, the institute acts in partnership with state government, higher education, and the private sector to promote alternatives to the violent resolution of conflict. It has programs on conflict resolution in schools, international conflict resolution, global education, international development, and world trade and sponsors many citizen exchange programs and joint projects.

Legacy International
128 N. Fayette St.
Alexandria, VA 22314
(703) 549-3630
Ira Kaufman, executive director
Committed to furthering prospects for peace and reconciliation in the Middle East through its extensive Dialogue Program, Legacy International sponsors student exchanges, cross-cultural training, public education forums, and joint action projects.

Non-Violence International
PO Box 39127

Friendship Station, NW
Washington, DC 20016
T: (202) 244-0951   F: (202) 244-6396
This organization trains dissenting international groups on the techniques of nonviolent protest and publishes the quarterly newsletter *Frontline*, which reports on nonviolent actions throughout the world.

Overseas Development Council
1875 Connecticut Ave., NW
Suite 1012
Washington, DC 20009
(202) 234-8701
The council's purpose is to increase American interest and understanding of the economic and social problems confronting the developing countries.

Oxfam America
26 West St.
Boston, MA 02111-1206
(617) 482-1211
Joel Charney, acting executive director
Oxfam America sponsors self-help development and disaster-relief projects in poor counties in Africa, Asia, Latin America, and the Caribbean and educates the American public on issues of hunger and development.

Pax World Service
1111 Sixteenth St., NW
Suite 120
Washington, DC 20036
(202) 293-7290
Larry Ekin, president
Pax promotes international understanding, reconciliation, and development by providing financial support to selected programs and projects. It sponsors friendship tours to the Middle East and elsewhere.

Peace Corps
1990 K St., NW
Washington, DC 20526
(202) 606-3010

The Peace Corps is a development-oriented, people-to-people program for friendship building and cultural exchange.

Peacelinks
729 Eighth St., SE
Suite 300
Washington, DC 20003
(202) 544-0805
Betty Bumpers, president
Peacelinks sponsors friendship tours and Pen Pals for Peace between women from the United States and the former Soviet Union. It encourages local initiatives for teaching and celebrating peace.

Physicians for Social Responsibility
1101 Fourteenth St., NW
Suite 700
Washington, DC 20005
(202) 898-0150
This organization is dedicated to educating the public and the medical profession about the threat of nuclear war.

Russian-American Center
2670 Leavenworth
San Francisco, CA 94133
(415) 292-8922
Rachel Radway, assistant director
This nonprofit organization addresses problems and opportunities shared by the peoples of Russia and the United States by promoting interaction between the governments and individuals of the two countries.

TransAfrica
1744 R St., NW
Washington, DC 20009
(202) 797-2301
Melissa Kemp, legislative director
TransAfrica is an educational resource offering constructive analysis of U.S. foreign policy as it affects the nations of Africa and the Caribbean.

20/20 Vision
1828 Jefferson Pl., NW

Washington, DC 20036
(202) 833-2020
Robin Caiola, codirector
This group's goal is to make democracy work to change U.S. military and environmental policy by removing obstacles that keep citizens from persistently lobbying policymakers. It encourages members to spend twenty minutes a month taking a single unified action determined by a local core group.

Track Five: Research, Training, and Education
Peacemaking through Learning

The primary task of the educational component of the Multi-Track Diplomacy system is to generate and transfer information about issues of peace and conflict, peacemaking and conflict resolution, and to suggest policy or action implications arising from that information. The assumption is that the more we study and learn, the more capable we are of collectively and concretely doing something about the enormous problems that face the planet. Another is that alternative ways of resolving conflicts are possible. Moreover, in order to change the world, we must begin by educating people.

Shape of the Field

This is a large subsystem with basically two different structural components: think tanks, including a variety of research, analysis, and study programs; and educational institutions—K–12, colleges, and universities—offering instruction in peace and conflict resolution issues. Training, educational events, research, and action programs can be found throughout both settings.

Think tanks range from the multimillion-dollar, abundantly staffed, well-respected institutions of bipartisan study to one-person, single-issue, single-publication offices. School programs in global education, cross-cultural studies, peace studies, world order studies, peer mediation, and conflict resolution abound throughout the country. Opportunities for degrees or degree concentrations in these subjects exist in over 300 colleges and universities. There are as yet few centers devoted exclusively to training in these fields; most of the training occurs within other programs, as does basic, applied, and action research.

There are several professional associations in this field: the Peace Studies Association, which serves the peace and conflict resolution programs in higher education; the National Association for Mediation in Education, which supports the teaching and practice of mediation in the schools; and the International Peace Research Association and its U.S. branch, the Consortium on Peace Research, Education and Development, which encourage research in the field and serve the research community.

Culture

Academia is a culture that values knowledge and rigorous, scientific means of obtaining and showing proficiency in a subject. Although the "science" of peace and conflict resolution is a soft one—that is, not a physical science with hypotheses provable in the laboratory, but one that deals with the unpredictable and unreasonable behavior of human beings—programs in the field tend to be academically rigorous. Students and teachers alike are challenged to work with their heads, not just their hearts, although caring and compassion are valued and there is a certain zeal and sense of mission about the subject.

Since the larger academic community is one in which competition for jobs and prestige, bureaucratic red tape, rigid requirements for tenure, and scarcity of funds are the norm, the peace and conflict resolution segment of that community also suffers from these constraints. However, as most peace and conflict studies programs are interdisciplinary, they also entail a certain sense of freedom, creativity, and innovation.

The think tank world is also a highly intellectual one, where knowledge is the premier value. It too can be bureaucratic in nature and tightly structured. Both of these communities tend to be dominated by white males, although more women are taking advanced degrees in the field and should be more strongly represented in the next generation of professionals.

The school programs have a different flavor. They are more overtly humanitarian oriented, more visibly value driven. Although schools can also be bureaucratic, they offer a looser structure for innovation, one that is better able to respond to community need or pressure. Then too, the world of children is a much looser, more spontaneous environment than the serious realm of academia. Regardless of the differences in setting, however, all the elements of this track share the goal of improving people's lives through learning, and all share an idealism and optimism that informed action can make a difference.

Activities

Think tanks engage in a large number of activities. They do research and analysis of situations, subjects, regions, or particular conflicts and may convene study groups, conferences, seminars, or workshops to both do their exploration and share their results. Results are also communicated through all kinds of publications: reports, newsletters, books, journals, papers, monographs, and articles. Think tank personnel may make videos or appear on television or radio shows to give commentary.

In an attempt to both gather wisdom and share it, think tanks bring people together from business, politics, academia, the military, and government for briefings, background, off-the-record dialogues, or advice. They develop conceptual and strategic models, undertake extensive projects of action and research, and make policy recommendations to decision makers. They often have access to Track One people and seek to inform and influence leaders and, to a lesser extent, the public.

Academic programs overlap the think tank world somewhat, in that they also do research, analysis, and publication and media commentary, especially graduate programs at large universities; they also hold conferences, seminars, and workshops. But academic programs have a strong instructional component that requires more attention to curriculum development, pedagogical studies, and faculty education, along with actual classes for students.

College programs usually have a community orientation, with public lectures, films, forums, and celebrations offered to the collegiate and surrounding communities. They may also offer training programs. Less focused on policy, colleges give more attention to the process of learning, to developing methodologies along with conceptual models, and to practical skills. Rather than seeking to influence leadership, academic institutions try to develop it.

One interesting phenomenon in the college community is the attention of the Hewlett Foundation to the field of conflict resolution. Since 1984, thirteen major universities have received ongoing institutional support to develop the theory and practice of conflict resolution. Although the schools have widely different approaches and focus on different topics, they form a subsystem within the whole, a kind of mini-community, and are trying to cross-fertilize one another's work and take on collaborative projects whenever possible.

Activities in the lower schools range from short single-class curriculum units to district-wide programs. Developing these units and creating the teaching materials are as much a part of the work as the actual instruction. Many schools have in-house mediation training and on-site programs with student mediators, so that conflict resolution is not merely a theoretical possibility but an immediate practice. The Iowa Peace Institute in Grinnell, Iowa, launched the first statewide program in the United States in 1989 and trained 3,000 teachers in peer mediation over the next four years. These are relatively new approaches in public schools, so there is still a lot of time and effort going into creating and evaluating such programs. Sharing the results with other schools is a new activity, although the National Association for Mediation in Education and other programs are becoming resources for that purpose.

Issues in the Field

Some of the issues facing the educational community are substantive: How do we pursue justice without violence and rectify past wrongs without inflicting new wounds? Which policies are the right ones for addressing our serious political, economic, and environmental challenges and dealing with the rapid currents of global change? Can we articulate a viable and commonly accepted theory of human behavior that allows us to prevent and anticipate conflicts and resolve them before they become violent? Once we help parties to a conflict identify their fundamental issues and needs, then what; who will deal with them? How do we get disputants to ask for or accept help? What are suitable nonviolent strategies, and how can we test them on a large scale? Can we turn our attention to domestic conflicts, learning about and applying our internationally oriented methodologies to local ethnic, racial, religious, and class conflicts and to the structural violence that pervades our society?

Other issues are more institutional and internal: How can we define our vocabulary more clearly so that we can communicate with one another and with other tracks better? How can we ensure financial and institutional stability and credibility and break down disciplinary and bureaucratic barriers? Where are the jobs in this field, and how can we deal with the tension between the personal and academic interests of both teachers and students and the need for job training? How can we strengthen our research into job opportunities and placement and develop new career possibilities?

How do we individualize the teaching programs to be more relevant to students' needs? Can we, should we teach more experientially and provide training in interpersonal and group skills, along with intellectual and analytical modes? What is the right balance between theory and practice, and between domestic and international focus? How can we link the subject of peace and conflict resolution with our own lives?

This is a particularly vibrant component of the Multi-Track Diplomacy community. Intellectual ferment and creativity are flourishing; students are pouring into study programs. This is the community from which much of the conflict resolution theory and practice is coming; this is where the exciting and often revolutionary learning for children of all ages is happening. People come from all over the world to America's research and education centers and then go home and seek to re-create what they have experienced here.

The educational track challenges our most basic worldview, our assumptions. It asks us to look deep into our own hearts and the heart of our most pressing world problems. Not having the operational responsibility that Track One has, thinkers and educators can enjoy the creative freedom to explore, grow, expand, synthesize, build, delve deeply, consider options, probe, invent, and inspire. Translating the richness of this work to the practitioners and policymakers is both a challenge and an opportunity for the whole Multi-Track Diplomacy system.

Place in the Field

Track Five is the brain of the system; it serves as the intellect or mind function for the whole. It analyzes, synthesizes, and produces information for the rest of the system—information on which the rest of the system depends. It also provides a continuity function by ensuring that ensuing generations are educated and brought into the new information age. In this way, the educational system plays a parental role, acting to ensure the evolution and survival of future generations.

The negative potential of this component is that the information it produces can be seen as an end in itself rather than as a foundation or tool for action. Also, information—being a primary resource to the functioning of the system—can, like any resource, be hoarded, manipulated, or otherwise used for power and advantage.

The positive aspect of Track Five is the wealth and richness of its contribution to the whole system. Brilliant minds are probing complex and intricate issues and finding, discovering, uncovering, and creating powerful and useful insights and information that can be translated into action that is beneficial to the world community. The training of the young, too, is an essential contribution to the whole.

Resources

Antioch College
Yellow Springs, OH 45387
(513) 767-6331
Contact: Paul Smoker or Maire Dugan
An important new peace studies and conflict resolution center is being developed at Antioch, with undergraduate and master's-level curricula.

Elise Boulding
University of Colorado
624 Pearl
Boulder, CO 80302
(303) 449-1617
Boulding is a pioneer and respected elder in peace research and education. She is past general secretary of the International Peace Research Association.

Brookings Institution
1775 Massachusetts Ave., NW

Washington, DC 20036
(202) 797-6000
Devoted to the analysis of significant public policy, Brookings has
research programs in economic, foreign policy, and governmental
studies; outreach through the Center for Public Policy Education;
and extensive publications.

Carnegie Commission on Preventing Deadly Conflict
2400 N St., NW, 6th floor
Washington, DC 20037
T: (202) 429-7979   F: (202) 429-9291
Jane E. Holl, executive director
The commission addresses the looming threats to world peace from
intergroup violence and advances new ideas about the prevention and
resolution of deadly conflict. It examines the principal causes of
deadly ethnic, nationalist, and religious conflicts within and between
states and the circumstances that foster or deter their outbreak.

Carnegie Endowment for International Peace
2400 N St., NW
Washington, DC 20037
(202) 862-7900
This group conducts research, discussion, publication, and education programs in international relations and U.S. foreign policy.

Center for Defense Information
1500 Massachusetts Ave., NW
Washington, DC 20005
(202) 862-0700
Eugene Carroll, deputy director
The center makes informative, independent appraisals of military
developments available to the public. It opposes excess and waste
in military spending and programs that increase the danger of
nuclear war. It offers extensive publications and public education.

Center for International Development and Conflict Management
University of Maryland
Tydings Hall Room 0145
College Park, MD 20742
(301) 314-7709
John Davies, research coordinator

A think tank on the management and resolution of protracted conflict, the center is developing the Global Event-Data Project, a computerized data system coding all newsworthy events for nation-states and all major ethnic groups and international organizations. It also has the Minorities at Risk Project—identifying major ethnic groups around the world that are politically active and vulnerable.

Center for International Policy
236 Massachusetts Ave., NE
Washington, DC 20002
(202) 544-4666
This is a nonprofit education and research organization concerned with U.S. policy toward the Third World and its impact on human rights and human needs.

Center for National Policy
1 Massachusetts Ave., NW
Suite 333
Washington, DC 20001
(202) 682-1800
Maureen Steinbruner, president
The center is dedicated to developing alternative policy proposals and approaches to governance.

Center for National Security Negotiations
1710 Goodridge Dr.
McLean, VA 22101
(703) 821-4583
Contact: Jackie Dedekind, Mailstop 1-9-3
The center provides policymakers and decision makers with sources of ideas and information to draw on in formulating effective negotiating strategies that support U.S. defense and foreign policy goals.

Center for Psychology and Social Change
1493 Cambridge St.
Cambridge, MA 02139
(617) 497-1553
Mary Ellen Hynes, acting director
This is a research and public education organization committed to the interdisciplinary study of the psychological dimensions of the global crisis generated by the arms race and the destruction of the

environment. It sponsors several projects on children's political world, conflict resolution and communication, decision making and policy, and the psychology of environmental responsibility.

Center for Strategic and International Studies
1800 K St., NW
Suite 400
Washington, DC 20006
(202) 887-0200
Joseph Montville, head of conflict resolution program
This is a think tank to advance the understanding of emerging world issues by providing a strategic perspective to decision makers that is integrative, international, anticipatory, and bipartisan.

Center for Teaching Peace
4501 Van Ness St., NW
Washington, DC 20016
(202) 537-1372
Coleman McCarthy, founder and director
The center provides public and in-school education on nonviolent approaches to life and peace.

Community Nonviolence Resource Center
2061 N. Los Robles Ave.
Suite 202
PO Box 40378
Pasadena, CA 91114-7378
T/F: (818) 398-0181
Ariel Bailey, executive director
This information, education, and training program is guided by the belief that the only way to create peace is to create peacemakers with a global perspective on violence and the prejudices that often inspire it. It is dedicated to actively building communities based on nonviolence, collaboration, justice, and respect for human diversity.

Conflict Research Consortium
University of Colorado
Campus Box 327
Boulder, CO 80309-0327
(303) 492-1635
Guy Burgess and Heidi Burgess, codirectors

This informal association of university organizations and individuals does work in the field of conflict resolution. It coordinates interdisciplinary research, gives small grants to conflict resolution projects, and sponsors programs to exchange information and develop proposals.

Conflict Resolution Center International
2205 E. Carson St.
Pittsburgh, PA 15203-2107
T: (412) 481-5559   F: (412) 481-5601
Contact: Paul Wahrhaftig
The center provides a network for international practitioners through its quarterly newsletter *Conflict Resolution Notes.*

Consortium on Peace Research, Education and Development
George Mason University
4103 Chainbridge Rd., 3rd floor
Fairfax, VA 22030-4444
(703) 273-4486
Barbara Wien, executive director
COPRED brings together researchers, educators, and activists working for a peaceful resolution of conflict and sponsors a major annual conference. It serves as the U.S. arm of the International Peace Research Association (IPRA).

Eastern Mennonite University Master's Program
   in Conflict Analysis and Transformation
1200 Park Rd.
Harrisonburg, VA 22801-2462
(703) 432-4452 or 4490
This program provides the connection between the classroom and the students' field experience. Through links with organizations engaged in peacebuilding in other regions of the world, such as the Nairobi Peace Initiative in Kenya and Justa Paz in Bogota, Colombia, the students are able to test their new understandings and skills in the various facets of peacebuilding, including conflict resolution, humanitarian relief, crisis management, and international development, gained in the master's program.

Albert Einstein Institution
50 Church St.

Cambridge, MA 02138
(617) 876-0311
Gene Sharp, president
This institution supports research, writing, and work on strategic uses of nonviolent sanctions in relation to problems of political violence.

Five College Program in Peace and World Security Studies
c/o Hampshire College
PO Box 50001
Amherst, MA 01002-5001
(413) 549-4600
Michael Klare, director
This multidisciplinary program among Smith, Mount Holyoke, Amherst, and Hampshire Colleges and the University of Massachusetts is intended to stimulate interest in the search for solutions to critical international problems.

Harvard Negotiation Project
Harvard Law School
Pound Hall, Room 512
Cambridge, MA 02138
(617) 495-1684
Roger Fisher, director
The project works to improve the theory, teaching, and practice of negotiation and dispute resolution so that people can deal more constructively with conflicts ranging from the interpersonal to the international. It offers education and research, theory building, intervention, and learning materials.

Institute for Conflict Analysis and Resolution
George Mason University
4400 University Dr.
Fairfax, VA 22030-4444
(703) 993-1300
Kevin Clements, director
The institute provides master's and Ph.D. programs in conflict analysis and resolution. It uses research, education, theory building, and Track Two conflict resolution to advance the understanding of deep-rooted conflict and its resolution.

Institute for International Economics
11 Dupont Circle, NW
Suite 620
Washington, DC 20036
(202) 328-9000
Louise Baker, office manager
The institute is involved in the study and discussion of international economic policy. Its publications seek to provide fresh analysis of key economic issues and to recommend new approaches for strengthening public policy toward them.

Institute for Multi-Track Diplomacy
Professional Development Program
1819 H St., NW
Suite 1200
Washington, DC 20006
T: (202) 466-4605   F: (202) 466-4607
IMTD's program exists to provide high-quality training and education to professionals in the many fields related to peacemaking and peacebuilding. Each program is intended to introduce participants to the latest theories and practices of Multi-Track Diplomacy in action and a systems approach to conflict resolution and peace.

Institute for Resource and Security Studies
27 Ellsworth Ave.
Cambridge, MA 02139
(617) 491-5177
The institute provides research and public education on the efficient use of natural resources for the protection of the environment and the furtherance of international peace and security.

Institute for the Study of Diplomacy
Georgetown University School of Foreign Service
Washington, DC 20057
(202) 965-5735
Charles Dogus, director of programs
The institute disseminates knowledge of the diplomatic process and its pivotal role in international peacemaking through studies and publications.

Institute of World Affairs
1321 Pennsylvania Ave., S.E.

Washington, DC 20003
T: (202) 544-4141   F: (202) 544-5115
Contact: Brad Johnson
The institute's work focuses on helping the international diplomatic community address the challenges faced by a rapidly changing world after the Cold War. It holds regular training sessions for midlevel diplomats that explore the latest theories of conflict, conflict resolution, negotiation, and mediation.

International Peace Academy
777 United Nations Plaza, 4th floor
New York, NY 10017-3521
(212) 949-8480
Devoted to the promotion of peace and the resolution of international and internal conflicts, the academy sponsors research, training, and education for international peacekeeping and peacemaking and behind-the-scenes workshops.

International Peace Research Association
Antioch College
Yellow Springs, OH 45387
(513) 767-6444
Paul Smoker, secretary-general
The association encourages worldwide cooperation to advance interdisciplinary research into the conditions of peace and the causes of war and other forms of violence.

Spark M. Matsunaga Institute for Peace
University of Hawaii
2424 Maile Way, Porteus 717
Honolulu, HI 96822
(808) 956-7427
Louann Guanson, director
Designed to develop and share knowledge about the root causes of violence, the conditions of peace, and the use of nonviolent means for resolving conflicts, the institute offers graduate and undergraduate peace studies curriculum, research, outreach, and Asia-Pacific dialogue.

MIT-Harvard Public Disputes Program
Harvard Law School

Pound Hall, Room 512
Cambridge, MA 02138
(617) 495-1684
Deborah Kolb, director
This program seeks to replace "win-lose" outcomes with "all-gain" solutions in the arena of public policymaking. It is sponsoring the International Environmental Negotiation Network to bring people together from many tracks in 160 countries and to monitor and improve the process of international environmental negotiation.

National Association for Mediation in Education
University of Massachusetts
205 Hampshire House
PO Box 33635
Amherst, MA 01003-3635
(413) 545-2462
Jack Seery, director
This international association of education administrators, trainers, and consultants is involved in school-based mediation and conflict resolution programs. It is a clearinghouse for information pertinent to the field.

National Institute for Dispute Resolution
1726 M St., N.W.
Suite 500
Washington, DC 20036
T: (202) 466-4764   F: (202) 466-4769
Contact: Doug Harbit
The institute promotes the development of fair, effective, and efficient conflict resolution processes and programs; fosters the use of such processes and programs in new arenas—locally, nationally, and internationally; and stimulates innovative approaches to the productive resolution of future conflict.

National Peace Institute Foundation
1835 K St., NW
Suite 610
Washington, DC 20006
(202) 223-1770
Stephen Strickland, executive director

The foundation educates the public about the U.S. Institute of Peace and international conflict management and resolution. It coordinates the Alliance for Our Common Future.

NTL Institute of Behavioral Science
1240 N. Pitt St.
Alexandria, VA 22314
(703) 548-1500
Lennox Joseph, executive director
The institute provides professional training, consulting, and education in intergroup relations, conflict resolution, and systems change.

Peace and Conflict Resolution Studies Program
School of International Service
American University
4400 Massachusetts Ave., NW
Washington, DC 20016
(202) 885-1622,
Abdul Aziz Said, director
This program provides graduate and undergraduate peace and conflict resolution studies. It prepares students for creative participation in building a global society based on peace, freedom, justice, and a diminished level of violence.

Peace Studies Association
Earlham College
Drawer 105
Richmond, IN 47374-4095
(317) 983-1305
Contact: Dorothy Meredith
This is an organization of college and university academic programs for the study of peace, conflict, justice, and global security.

Resolving Conflict Creatively Program
163 Third Ave., #239
New York, NY 10003
(212) 260-6290
Sheila Alson, coordinator
This program is cosponsored by the New York City Board of Education/Office of Health, Physical Education and School Sports, and Educators for Social Responsibility, Metropolitan Area. It promotes

effective instruction in creative conflict resolution and intergroup relations in the New York City public schools.

School for International Training
Kipling Rd.
Box 1313
Brattleboro, VT 05320
(802) 258-3267
SIT offers a variety of degrees in international studies; its mission is to enable participants to develop the knowledge, skills, and attitudes needed to contribute effectively to international understanding and global development.

Society of Professionals in Dispute Resolution
815 Fifteenth St., NW
Suite 530
Washington, DC 20005
T: (202) 783-7277   F: (202) 783-7281
This international organization was founded in 1972 to advance and represent the interests of third-party neutrals who serve as dispute resolvers and to enhance the capacity of parties in conflict to achieve rational and equitable solutions without violence or litigation.

Southern Center for International Studies
320 West Paces Ferry Rd., NW
Atlanta, GA 30305
(404) 261-5763
Cedric Suzman, vice president and educational program director
The center seeks to educate businesses, academicians, journalists, state government officials, and the public about world events so that they may make better decisions. It sponsors annual gatherings of all living secretaries of state, secretaries of defense, and UN ambassadors.

Stanley Foundation
216 Sycamore St.
Suite 500
Muscatine, IA 52761
(319) 264-1500
The foundation sponsors conferences on U.S. foreign policy and United Nations issues, congressional staff training, citizen involvement in peacemaking, and security studies.

United States Institute of Peace
1550 M St., NW
Washington, DC 20005
(202) 457-1700
Eileen Babbit, training and education director
Created by the U.S. government to provide research, training, education, and peace information services on the means of promoting international peace and conflict resolution, the institute offers grants, public educational forums, conferences, training, and a library program.

World Orders Models Project
475 Riverside Dr.
Room 246
New York, NY 10115
(212) 870-2391
This international association of scholars, intellectuals, and political activists is engaged in resolution, education, dialogue, and action to promote a just world order.

World Policy Institute
65 Fifth Ave.
Suite 413
New York, NY 10003
(212) 229-5808
The institute is engaged in the formulation and promotion of public policy recommendations on U.S. and international economic and security issues.

World Without War Council
1730 Martin Luther King Jr. Way
Berkeley, CA 94709
(510) 845-1992
Robert Pickus, president
The council's goal is to make the United States a leader in programs that resolve international conflict without war in a way that contributes to the growth of free societies and the well-being of our own.

Track Six: Activism
Peacemaking through Advocacy

The primary task of the activist community is to change institutions, attitudes, and policies through political action. It is based on the assumption that peace is not possible without social, political, environmental, and economic justice and integrity. In this subsystem, citizens are believed to have the moral duty to actively oppose unwise policies and injustice and to support and secure the rights and well-being of all who are oppressed.

Like Track Four, private citizens, the activist community believes that grassroots action and leadership are critical. Activism is a mass movement. Unlike citizen diplomacy, which focuses on increasing understanding, activism concentrates on bringing to light and working to oppose those actions and policies that it sees as immoral, oppressive, or detrimental to peace with justice.

Shape of the Field

One way to look at the activist community is by topic. Groups tend to form around specific issues such as peace and justice, the environment, war, militarism, disarmament, and human rights. Another perspective is by size. This field includes major transnational organizations such as Amnesty International, which has over a million members globally; national organizations such as Peace Action (formerly Sane/Freeze) that have chapters throughout the United States; and local organizations such as the Washington Peace Center. Most organizations have members or at least supporters who contribute not only much of the funding but also the participants in public actions. The field also includes individuals who are not necessarily associated with any group or those who are affiliated with many and participate in actions on specific topics.

The activist community has its own funding sources. Certain individuals and foundations prefer to fund grassroots activist projects. There are also businesses that support the funding process and become involved in activist business and environmental causes. There is significant overlap with the religious community and with private citizen advocacy, development, and exchange groups.

Culture

The activist world is highly value driven. It defines itself as humanitarian, seeking those human connections that enable us to transcend our differences and invoke moral conscience to guide our behavior toward others. It is justice oriented and, with the exception of a few organizations, is committed to nonviolence and respect for all life and life-forms. It sees itself as upholding a righteous struggle against violence, greed, cruelty, inhumaneness, and the oppression of people's basic rights and dignity. It abhors the abuse of power and promotes self-empowerment.

The activist track is based ultimately on compassion and on moral indignation. It is a field in which physical courage and the courage of conscience are frequently necessary, since activists often practice civil disobedience and go to jail.

Unlike many of the other tracks, activists tend to value and express the emotional side of their peace work. Profound anger and joyful exuberance, and every human emotion in between, are openly expressed, and both argumentation and overt demonstrations of love and caring are common. The organizational culture is generally informal in dress and speech. Women are plentiful in the field, though men still run most of the major organizations. The field seeks ethnic diversity but is still more predominantly white than it would like to be.

This is one place in the multi-track system where people of all ages regularly interact; in fact, this is a field where generational continuity exists. Many who are currently active attended their first rallies or demonstrations in their mothers' wombs, and it is not unusual for three generations of families to march or protest together.

One of the values that distinguishes this community from some of the others is its heavy reliance on collective and cooperative action.

Coalitions and alliances are the way of life; groups overlap in membership, interest, and values and rarely work alone. The concept of solidarity is crucial—solidarity with the oppressed, with those of like intention. This is a track that knows the value of, and uses, networking as a way of getting things done.

Activities

The activities of this track fall under six main categories: protest, education, advocacy, organizing, support, and witnessing. The tools for protest are many and include rallies, demonstrations, marches, vigils, hunger strikes, boycotts, and local or national campaigns. Educationally, activist groups may sponsor teach-ins, seminars, conferences, forums, meetings, training, research, and tabling (the setting up of tables at local events with literature and people available to discuss the issues with passersby). To advocate certain positions, activist groups mount petition drives and letter-writing campaigns, lobby decision makers, do media education and commentary, mobilize mass citizen action, and activate legislative alerts.

Because so much of the work in this field is at the grassroots level, one of its major activities concerns organizing its constituents. Its strength depends on its ability to educate and mobilize citizens, so much of its attention goes toward that process. This is also a major subject for training within the community; how to organize and maintain the activated constituency is an art. One way to keep people energized and inspired is through music. Track Six has many musicians who perform at rallies, concerts, and fund-raisers and who involve people through the power of sound and song.

The system also knows how to work with the elite, those who make the decisions and those who influence the opinions of policymakers and the public. Sophisticated methodologies exist in this track for one-on-one relationship building and networking. All the major organizations in the field have, like the think tanks, their key contacts in the government, the media, and other high places and know how to work the system to maximize their influence. Sometimes, especially in the case of those activist organizations that are international in scope, this leads to quiet, behind-the-scenes citizen diplomacy, which can play a significant role in peacemaking or peacebuilding, particularly during a crisis.

The support work undertaken by the system consists of direct aid and programs of education, training, and empowerment offered to the populations in whose cause the activists are participating. Health, housing, business, agricultural, political, and legal assistance is often made available to refugees in the United States as well as in-country to those suffering from the injustices activists seek to redress.

This system uses the witnessing process as a tool to affect policy. Witness programs send American citizens to war zones to serve as deterrents to violence through their very presence, or to witness and report back the political and human rights abuses they see. Witnessing also changes those who do it; being in the midst of a conflict or potential conflict, often living with the local people, changes the view of even the most educated and pragmatic American by making the human effects of our policies immediate and real.

Additionally, this is a community that knows how to have fun. It often raises money, increases its visibility, and strengthens community connections through dinners, concerts, fairs, auctions, and festivals. It is also a system with its own natural business outlets: many peace centers have stores, street booths, or catalogues to sell bumper stickers, pins, educational materials, clothing, games, and other items from the Third World or that address politically appropriate themes.

Issues in the Field

The worldview of the activist community is a coherent whole, so that people who, for example, feel angry about U.S. military aid to El Salvador will likely oppose deforestation policies and nuclear weapons testing. Although this cohesion can be a strength, it can also be a detriment to the system, imposing what has come to be called a mantle of "politically correct" thinking that allows for little divergence.

Although values and assumptions are commonly shared, strategies and tactics are not. These differences form the basis for many in-house conflicts, especially when alliances and coalitions of groups work together. Argument and conflict within and among groups are not uncommon, and conflict resolution is a skill that has not yet made its way firmly into this community. People want action, not process; feeling the rightness of their cause, they want to do something, not talk about how to do it or how they feel.

That certitude and clarity of intention allows for fast and strong action. This community can mobilize thousands of people on short notice for a single campaign, march, or project, and its actions can have a significant impact on the political awareness and will of the public and the nation's leadership.

Activists frequently feel themselves caught in the middle between two major pressures. On one side stands an apathetic citizenry that doesn't always feel a personal, immediate connection with international events. On the other stands a government that is apparently seeding disinformation and promulgating destructive policies while actively harassing and denigrating the activists who seek to correct the situation. The frustration level can get very high, and the sense of helplessness is never far away. On top of that, activists are dealing, often directly and intimately, with abused and oppressed populations suffering great pain. Making the government "the enemy" becomes easy, and keeping the heart open to hope and the ears open to hearing other points of view is difficult.

Another challenge facing this field is its lack of power in the larger system. For instance, when President Bush used the Amnesty International report on Iraq's human rights abuses in Kuwait to justify his strong commitment to defending Kuwait, he got major media coverage. But Amnesty International was unable to get any coverage to explain how the president had misrepresented some of its findings and failed to put them in the context of other reports, a context that would have significantly changed the impact of the president's message.

Activists are not particularly popular outside their own community. They labor under the burden of derogatory and derisive labels, such as "peacenik," and are frequently branded as unpatriotic or worse. They have been the subject of harassment from individuals, police, public officials, and the FBI.

The issues facing the activist community are the same as those facing the other tracks, but with a twist. This field is dealing not only with ethnic conflict in the Third World but also with the U.S. role in perpetrating the conditions that lead to that conflict. It is considering environmental threats to health and safety as well as the government policies that encourage environmental degradation and hinder the elimination of the threat. Like the rest of the Multi-Track Diplomacy community, activists are discovering that organizations and projects that made sense even three years ago now seem outdated and are in the process of reorganizing and restructuring.

The Persian Gulf War introduced a new element into the activist community. Many who had long histories of protest, demonstration, and antiwar action found that the old forms, based on anger, no longer worked for them. Throughout the country, small, informal groups met to find new ways to explore their own ambivalence, to open their hearts to the victims of war (including the soldiers), or to express their strong opposition to the war in creative ways that were not so polarizing. Many tapped into the relationship of conflict in the larger world to that in their own lives and used the opportunity to refocus on unresolved issues in their families and workplaces.

What enables the activist community to be effective is the incredible sincerity and commitment of its members and the widespread, grassroots networks that exist to support the work. Like the other tracks that have networks in place on the ground in conflict areas around the world, Track Six activists have a profound knowledge of the intricacies of people's lives, how they are affected by events and policies, and the underlying needs being expressed in conflict situations. This knowledge could and should be more available to the whole system, if the system were open to all its collective wisdom.

Place in the Field

Track Six is the fight leader of the system. It opposes that which is inhumane or ineffective in the rest of the system and draws public and leadership attention to the need to correct what is wrong. It provides a necessary counterbalance to Track One by making sure that it does not act entirely unrestrainedly, without checks on its propensity to abuse power.

The negative side of the activist role is that, by defining itself primarily as anti, or against, something, it runs the risk of escalating or strengthening the very force against which it is pushing. By acting frequently in a mode based on anger, this track feeds conflict and adversarial thinking, which, although useful at times, tends to lock people into positions rather than foster communication and synthesis. In fact, this anger may so alienate Track One officials that they respond counterproductively, in ways that bring negative consequences to other tracks of the system.

The positive side of Track Six is that it champions the unrepresented, the invisible, and the marginalized of the human system and holds our feet to the fire to ensure that we do not ignore our responsibility to see the effects of our behavior and to meet the needs of all.

Resources

Amnesty International
304 Pennsylvania Ave., SE
Washington, DC 20003
(202) 544-0200
Jim O'Dea, director
This office serves as the Washington office of this transnational organization which tries to document human rights abuses with credibility and without bias. Amnesty International exerts pressure on U.S. and foreign governments to correct specific human rights violations and improve human rights policies.

CISPES (Committee in Solidarity with the People of El Salvador)
PO Box 1801
New York, NY 10160
T: (212) 229-1290   F: (212) 645-7280
Cherrene Horazuk, executive director
CISPES consists of dozens of grassroots chapters in communities across the United States. Since 1980, it has supported El Salvador's democratic revolutionary movement and has challenged and changed U.S. government policy toward Central America.

Human Rights Watch
485 Fifth Ave.
New York, NY 10017-6104
T: (212) 972-8400   F: (212) 972-0905
Kenneth Roth, executive director
HRW conducts regular, systematic investigations of human rights abuses in some seventy countries around the world. It addresses the human rights practices of governments of all political stripes, geopolitical alignments, and ethnic and religious persuasions. In internal wars, it documents violations by both governmental and rebel

groups. HRW demands freedom of thought and expression, due process, and equal protection of the law.

IF
3015 Freedom Blvd.
Lake Freedom
Watsonville, CA 95076
(408) 724-5526
This longtime activist and educational organization fosters hopeful alternatives for people within contemporary social structures and publishes *Integrities* magazine on a quarterly basis. It is particularly active in Central America.

Robin Lloyd
c/o Toward Freedom
209 College St.
Burlington, VT 05401
(802) 658-2523
Lloyd is a longtime activist, filmmaker, and community catalyst, as well as publisher of *Toward Freedom*, an international news analysis and advocacy journal.

Peace Action Education Fund
1819 H St., NW
Washington, DC 20006-3640
(202) 862-9740
Contact: Ira Schorr
This national membership organization of activists seeks to shift dollars from the military budget to human needs and a peace economy. It was highly visible and effective during anti–Vietnam War and antinuclear movements as Sane and Sane/Freeze.

Peace and Justice Center
21 Church St.
Burlington, VT 05401
(802) 863-2345
The center is a coalition of area groups that work together to inform and empower themselves and the community, convinced that a just and peaceful world is possible. The coalition provides three main resources: the Peace and Justice Center, a resource library; a Peace on

Earth Store, which sells products that promote social responsibility and cultural understanding; and the *Peace and Justice News*, a monthly newsletter.

Resource Center for Nonviolence
515 Broadway
Santa Cruz, CA 95060
(408) 423-1626
The center offers educational programs about nonviolence as a force for personal and social change. It promotes cooperation with nonviolent movements throughout Latin America and the Middle East.

Molly Scott
c/o Sumitra Productions, Inc.
Box U
Charlemont, MA 01339
(413) 339-4245
Scott is a musician and leads workshops in the transformational power of sound. She writes and sings music about peace and justice.

South Dakota Peace and Justice Center
PO Box 405
Watertown, SD 57201
(605) 882-2822
The center seeks to make peace between Native Americans and whites and between the people and Mother Earth. It focuses on Native American rights, reconciliation, disarmament, and environmentally and socially sound economic development.

Washington Peace Center
2111 Florida Ave., NW
Washington, DC 20008
(202) 234-2000
The center provides peace and justice education and action in the Washington metropolitan area.

Witness for Peace
110 Maryland Ave., NE

Suite 311
Washington, DC 20002-5611
T: (202) 544-0781   F: (202) 544-1187
Witness for Peace sends volunteers to establish a continuous international presence in Central American communities where life is
at risk. It brings the facts about U.S. policies in Central America to
the U.S. media, Congress, and the North American people.

Track Seven: Religion
Peacemaking through Faith in Action

The religious community seeks to bring the moral laws and spiritual truths of God and the universe to the practical establishment of peace on earth. Religious groups of diverse persuasions believe that they naturally belong on the forefront of work for peace and justice, understanding and reconciliation, because, in their belief systems, these issues are at the heart of humanity's spiritual evolution. They feel compelled by their faith to bring their consciences into service and action for the benefit of all people.

Several basic assumptions underlie this work, key among them being a strong belief in the unity or oneness of the human family. Another is that love and compassion are the means by which that unity becomes manifest and by which people become able to find peace and resolve conflict. A third is that peace exists as our divine birthright and grows from within the inner experience of the individual to encompass our relationships with one another and with the earth itself. Peace is seen as an inherent divine gift or quality: it is our sacred duty to bring it forth.

Shape of the Field

Groups from many different religious and spiritual persuasions are active in peace work at the local, national, and international levels. We considered some of them from the following streams: Catholic, Evangelical Protestant, mainstream Protestant, Jewish, Buddhist, Hindu, Baha'i, Native American, Quaker, Mennonite, and New Age. In addition, we looked at numerous interfaith and ecumenical groups and at think tanks or policy centers designed to bring the

97

religious perspective to the policymaking world or to study the role of religion in peacemaking.

This is a tremendously populous and diverse field, with everything from small local church groups, where a handful of concerned congregants study peace issues, to a major international conference center, where thousands from differing faiths gather yearly for dialogue. Unimaginable numbers of people around the globe make up the constituency of this system. The major churches and denominations have adherents and networks of active, willing members in virtually every corner of the world. Liberation theology alone has affected the major institutions and individual lives of thousands if not millions in Central and South America. Worldwide, the Jewish and Muslim communities watch the events of the ongoing Arab-Israeli conflict with concern. There is also the factor of historical continuity to consider: religious wars that are still being played out today have decades, even centuries, of historical antecedent; Quakers have been doing peace work for over 300 years.

Some of the elements of the religious community are highly visible in the Multi-Track Diplomacy system, such as the public letters issued by Catholic or Methodist bishops to guide their congregants. Others are less visible but well known, such as the presence of American Friends Service Committee representatives on the ground in many major conflict areas. Still others are nearly invisible and unknown, such as the ancient teachings of Native American cultures on peace and governance. Several components of this subsystem are outside the experience of mainstream American society altogether—for example, the work of the maharishi field theory of consciousness or the teachings of the ageless wisdom—but they are nonetheless relevant and important pieces of the whole.

Culture

This is a community that has an active vision of peace, of what a world of peace would look like. It has a sense of mission and sees its role as transformational. Some of the norms and values expressed throughout the system include a belief in and commitment to such things as:

- The spiritual truth of the interconnectedness of all life;
- Social action;
- A prophetic imperative to seek justice, feed the hungry, heal the sick, and minister to the poor;
- Equality and justice;
- Forgiveness, contrition, and reconciliation;
- Practicing one's spiritual values in one's own life;
- Community, especially the "beloved community" Martin Luther King Jr. spoke of;
- Hospitality;
- Full and loving presence with the poor;
- The fostering of hope;
- Living with an open, loving, and compassionate heart;
- Nonviolence and, in some cases, pacifism;
- Caretaking of ourselves, one another, and all precious beings; and
- Service.

Like the activist community, with whom its activities often overlap, the religious community often seeks coalitions and alliances. Although within the religious community there are factions and infighting, there is also a high degree of cooperation, mutual respect, and ecumenism and an active spirit of healing.

The religious peace community is similar to the activist community in diversity as well: women are a strong presence, though less so at leadership levels, and people of color are active, though not as numerous as most groups would like.

Activities

The religious peace community undertakes many of the same functions found in other tracks: public and elite education, conferences, research, behind-the-scenes discussion and conflict mediation, dialogue projects, media commentary, protests, rallies, activist campaigns, publications, and relief and development work. Some of its activities, however, are unique or at least unusual: it engages in prayer and meditation as major tools of its work, it offers sanctuary to refugees, it raises ethical questions about national policy, it has an extensive United Nations presence through nongovernmental organizations, it offers training and education in nonviolence, and it offers its work through mission service and community involvement.

Interfaith dialogue and joint projects are an important aspect of the work of this community, as is religion-based travel and citizen exchange. In fact, much of its work has to do in one way or another with bringing people together to transcend their differences. It has widespread, established networks that are not often involved in the work of other tracks. In some cases, it provides extensive unofficial conflict resolution and conciliation services that never come to public attention. It works deeply with economic and social development issues, as well as with political issues.

Transformational politics is a phrase that has come from the spiritual community. It addresses the notion that our consciousness or worldview must change to address the issues of our times and that this change in consciousness must be embedded in our political decisions and institutions. Meditation and prayer groups now exist at the Pentagon and other major government departments. This is the component of the Multi-Track Diplomacy system that takes most to heart the adage "let peace begin with me." Probably nowhere else in the system are so many actively engaged with the work of finding peace in their own hearts and homes as a foundation for peace around the globe.

Issues in the Field

Some of the issues facing this community are, naturally, doctrinal or belief differences; some are operational. A major ongoing dialogue, recently brought to public attention, has to do with what constitutes a "just war," or if indeed there is any such thing. Pacifism, long the purview of the so-called peace churches (Quaker, Mennonite, and Church of the Brethren), is increasingly being expressed and argued in more mainstream denominations as well. In fact, whereas the peace churches were once the pioneers in overseas peace work, mainstream denominations are now increasingly active.

The role of churches in developing nations is still an issue. Traditional Catholicism, liberation theology, and Evangelical Protestantism are at odds with one another in their attempts to touch the lives of the masses in Central America and other Third World areas. Those debates continue here in this country through writing and dialogue.

As might be expected, the different denominations give their greatest attention to those areas of the world where they have the strongest presence. Because of the historical role of Christianity in Latin America, this area draws much attention from the Christian part of the religious peace community. The Israeli situation is the central focus of most of the Jewish groups. Buddhists tend to follow the situations in Asian countries, and Native Americans focus on indigenous peoples everywhere.

There are differences between the leadership and the membership of many religious groups. Often the leadership is publicly outspoken but the rank and file are quiet; sometimes it is the other way around, with local groups being active and their leadership silent. Some religious leaders believe that their communities are too involved in the social and economic fields and not enough in the political, especially in election and partisan politics. Some believe that the public and the policymakers have to be educated to understand the moral meaning of history, or the historical memory of wrongdoing and suffering carried into current conflicts from past events. People also need to be trained to think beyond their own needs for the good of the whole.

The moral impulse behind the actions of this community, its clear vision of peace, its openheartedness, and its tested ability to provide practical applications of the truths of natural law are some of the forces that make the work of this community so strong. Its widespread network of people of goodwill around the planet is another, along with its skills in conciliation and reconciliation. The community would probably say of itself that its greatest strength is the divine will and love that flow through its every action, of which it is simply an instrument, a vehicle for the realization of peace on earth.

Place in the Field

The religious community is the heart of the Multi-Track Diplomacy system. It provides the spiritual impulse, the idealism, and the ethical foundation that, though perhaps present elsewhere in the system, are most publicly and acceptably articulated here. Without an open heart, the system could not manage its ultimate aim: to relieve the suffering of humanity by bringing about a world of peace.

The negative potential within this component is its historical propensity for exclusivity. Although most of the activity of the religious community is in fact ecumenical and interfaith oriented, there are still those threads of thinking that say that only one way is the true way and that other paths are ultimately not only wrong but actually sinful or evil.

The positive aspect of this track is that it brings a higher dimension of understanding and feeling to the issues of war and peace. Unity, the underlying principle of all religion, expressed in love for all sisters and brothers of creation in their diversity and unique dignity, is the ultimate work of this track and the peace and conflict resolution community.

Resources

American Friends Service Committee
1501 Cherry St.
Philadelphia, PA 19102
(215) 241-7000
This Quaker organization sends representatives to conflict areas to serve as bridges of communication and reconciliation. It provides public education on nonviolent alternatives to conflict and militarization and aids refugees and war victims through emergency programs and long-term reconstruction and development projects.

Baha'i International Community
866 United Nations Plaza
Suite 120
New York, NY 10017-1811
(212) 756-3500
This international spiritual community is dedicated to world unity and working for peace through social and economic development throughout the world. It is a strong presence as an international nongovernmental organization at the United Nations.

Rabbi Balfour Brickner
Stephen Wise Synagogue
30 W. Sixty-eighth St.
New York, NY 10023
(212) 877-4050
One of the original cofounders of Clergy and Laity Concerned,
which played a powerful role in opposing the Vietnam War, Brickner
is a leading spokesman for Jewish social action for peace and justice.

Clergy and Laity Concerned
340 Mead Rd.
Decatur, GA 30030
(404) 377-1983
Carol Frazier, head of staff
This network of people of faith and conscience from all walks of
life is helping to build a movement for justice and peace. It is committed to work on issues of militarism, economic justice, human
rights, and racial justice.

Fellowship of Reconciliation
Box 271
Nyack, NY 10960
(914) 358-4601
Contact: Richard Deats
This international, interfaith organization and its local chapters
seek to build a world of peace for the whole human family. It orga-
nizes denominational fellowships (for example, the Buddhist
Peace Fellowship, Jewish Peace Fellowship) and promotes programs and action on peace, disarmament, and racial and economic
justice.

Foundation for a Global Community
222 High St.
Palo Alto, CA 94301-1097
(415) 328-7756
The foundation is dedicated to building a secure and sustainable
future through the practical application of the basic truths of interdependence of all life, diversity within unity, and nonviolent conflict
resolution. Originally a religious organization, it is now nonsectar-
ian, with chapters all around the country.

Alan Geyer
Wesley Theological Seminary
4500 Massachusetts Ave., NW
Washington, DC 20016
(202) 885-8600
Geyer is executive director of Churches' Center for Theology and
Public Policy and is a professor of political ethics and an ecumenicist.
He is deeply involved in issues of defense and disarmament.

Jewish Peace Fellowship
Box 271
Nyack, NY 10960
(914) 358-4601
Contact: Joyce Bressler
Committed to nonviolent social activism, the fellowship is working
to abolish war and create a community of concern transcending
national boundaries and selfish interests.

Martin Luther King Jr. Center for Nonviolent Social Change
449 Auburn Ave., NE
Atlanta, GA 30312
(404) 526-8948 or 1956
Based on the teachings of Martin Luther King Jr., the center is dedicated to teaching, interpreting, advocating, and promoting non-
violently the elimination of poverty, racism, violence, and war; it
provides training in nonviolence.

Maharishi International University
1000 N. Fourth St.
Fairfield, IA 52557-1026
(515) 472-7493
Contact: Pat Robinson, Box 1026
The university offers theory development and research in the maharishi technology of the unified field, a group meditation process
that aims to raise the level of coherence in collective consciousness,
thus providing a stable basis for lasting world peace.

Mennonite Central Committee
PO Box 500
Akron, PA 17501-0500
(717) 859-3889

The MCC is the voluntary service, relief, and development arm of the Mennonite and Brethren in Christ Churches of North America. It contains the Mennonite Conciliation Service, which was established to promote work in the area of conflict resolution and mediation, primarily in North America, and the International Conciliation Service to address and promote linkages between relief, development, and peacemaking in international settings.

Moral Re-Armament, Inc.
1156 Fifteenth St., NW
Suite 910
Washington, DC 20005-1704
(202) 872-9077
Richard Ruffin, director
MRA is a worldwide interfaith network of people who have accepted the principle that to change the world we must start with ourselves. It has had a profound effect on reconciliation between individuals, groups, and nations. MRA helps politicians find clear motives and creative ideas and sponsors local, regional, and international conferences, roundtable meetings, and international exchanges.

Joe Nangle, Executive Assistant
Sojourners
2401 Fifteenth St., NW
Washington, DC 20009
(202) 328-8842
Nangle assists the work of Sojourners, an ecumenical Bible-based movement that seeks to combine faith and political action. He was a Catholic missionary priest in South America for fifteen years, working with the poor through the principles of liberation theology.

NETWORK: A National Catholic Social Justice Lobby
801 Pennsylvania Ave., SE
Suite 460
Washington, DC 20003
(202) 547-5556
NETWORK works for just access to economic resources, fairness in national funding, and justice in global relationships.

Religious Action Center
2027 Massachusetts Ave., NW

Washington, DC 20036
(202) 387-2800
The center mobilizes the Jewish community in the nation's capital
for social justice and religious liberty.

Corinne McLaughlin and Gordon Davidson
Sirius Community
8306 Cathedral Forest Dr.
Fairfax Station, VA 22039
T: (703) 764-0999   F: (703) 764-5373
Coauthors of *Builders of the Dawn* and *Spiritual Politics*, McLaughlin
and Davidson are teachers of the ageless wisdom and transformational politics, applying the new paradigm to the political
world.

Soka Gakkai International–USA
4603 Eastern Ave.
Mt. Rainier, MD 20712-2407
T: (301) 779-3255   F: (301) 779-4954
Contact: Bill Aiken
This worldwide organization of Buddhist lay believers is dedicated
to peace, culture, and education. There is an emphasis on the pro-
motion of cultural and educational activities and exchanges.

Sunray Meditation Society
Box 308
Bristol, VT 05443
(802) 453-4610
Dhyani Ywahoo, director
The society brings the ancient wisdom on peace and peacemaking
of the Etowah Tsalagi (Cherokee) people to the public through educational programs and service projects; it sponsors "The Peace-
keeper Mission," an international peace education program.

Unitarian Universalist United Nations Office
777 United Nations Plaza, 7D
New York, NY 10017
(212) 986-5165
This group advances the Unitarian universalist ideals of international cooperation and world peace with justice through seminars
and annual conferences.

Weston Priory
58 Priory Hill Rd.
Weston, VT 05161
(802) 824-5409
Contact: Brothers Richard and Philip
This Benedictine monastic community sponsors retreats in Mexico to provide a loving and learning presence with the poor. It also supports solidarity with grassroots groups in Latin America and with the African American, Native American, and Appalachian communities. It offers sanctuary to Guatemalan refugee families, and its monastery is an embassy for human-to-human grassroots diplomacy.

World Conference on Religion and Peace
777 United Nations Plaza, 9th floor
New York, NY 10017
(212) 687-2163
Contact: William Vendley
This is a forum promoting interreligious encounters and cooperation throughout the world, working for peace through justice.

Track Eight: Funding
Peacemaking through Providing Resources

The primary task of the funding community is to provide financial support for the activities and institutions of the Multi-Track Diplomacy system. By choosing and setting guidelines for the activities it will fund, it essentially sets the agenda for the field, defining its critical issues and establishing priorities. It also serves as a gatekeeper, determining who will enter and gain visibility and credibility in the field and who will not.

The assumption on which the work of this community is based is that those with wealth have a responsibility and an opportunity to make a positive contribution to the world through the judicious use of that money to sponsor worthwhile projects. Also underlying much of philanthropy is the belief that the projects funded will explore critical issues, provide needed action, and contribute to the growth and evolution of humanity as it seeks a more peaceful world. In other words, foundations do not necessarily define their business as giving away money but more as exploring critical areas of knowledge and action.

Shape of the Field

This field has two distinguishable divisions. The large, mainstream foundations—such as the Ford Foundation, Pew Charitable Trust, MacArthur Foundation, Carnegie, Mott, and others—primarily fund major academic and research institutions whose interests lean toward area studies, security, and public policy issues. Smaller, progressive organizations—such as the Tides Foundation, Threshold, Plowshares, and others—appear to be more interested in grassroots action projects and are more likely to give to environmental, justice, anti-nuclear, and citizen empowerment programs. In addition, there are individuals who give their money independently or through small family foundations to whatever causes interest them. There are also foundations that do not give money per se but support the field by operational programs that provide resources and services to others, for example, the Stanley and Kettering Foundations.

Some foundations provide money for institutional support, such as the Hewlett and Winston Foundations, within which certain programs may be developed. Others fund only projects and allow for no institutional overhead. Two organizations, the Council on Foundations and ACCESS, provide some overview to the field. The former offers support services to all foundations, not just those in the peace and conflict resolution community. ACCESS publishes a guide to those foundations that are specifically interested in supporting this field.

Culture

The culture in this subsystem varies with the different components. The large foundations tend to be traditional bureaucratic systems, run by boards that are predominantly white and male. The smaller, progressive foundations are often more casual, drawing their staffs and boards from the activist, citizen diplomacy, and socially responsible business communities. They usually include more women and, although they are still mostly white, have a greater sensitivity to and interest in issues of ethnic diversity. The decision-making process in progressive foundations is also more likely to be consensual. Small family foundations operate within whatever particular style and culture the family prefers.

The values of this community are different, too, in that different priorities are stressed, but throughout the field there are strong commitments to making a more peaceful world, preventing nuclear war, and reducing or eliminating the use of arms as a method of solving problems. There is in this community a sense of service: funders often see themselves as serving those on the front lines who are increasing our collective knowledge and experimenting with new approaches. There is also a strong underlying value of generosity.

Activities

Foundations have different methods for getting proposals, deciding which ones to fund, and following up. Some have certain timelines, accepting proposals only at specified times of the year. Others are open to proposals on an ongoing basis. Some ask for a preliminary letter of inquiry; others have a formal and extensive application process. Some foundations have peer review procedures or outside readers. Others rely on their internal staffs for making decisions. Some require strict accounting and accountability for evaluating projects. Others have an informal evaluation process. Some fund the same institutions year after year; others do not.

Not all the foundations are ongoing endowments. Some solicit money from individual donors and other foundations that they then give out as grants. In these cases, much time and attention go toward identifying potential donors, building and maintaining relationships with them, and generating a larger financial base through ongoing solicitation. This process, though time-consuming, brings individual citizens into the process of funding in ways that are inclusive and empowering.

The gamut of issues funded by the field is as large as the field itself. Security studies probably lead the list, and today they include redefining security to cover environmental, population, health, and economic concerns as well as military ones. Alternative, collective, and nonoffensive security methods are being studied, especially as post–Cold War dynamics change the security situation. Also popular are issues relating to nuclear war—nonproliferation of nuclear weapons, arms control, and disarmament—although these are slowly shifting with the end of the Cold War. Increasing attention is being paid to encouraging and building democratic infrastructures in emerging democracies and to environmental problems as a major threat to world security.

Area studies and public policy issues receive substantial funding. Major foundations give much attention to projects that educate and influence policymakers and opinion makers, and some attention to training upcoming scholars and specialists.

Other topics funded consistently, mostly by the progressive foundations, include grassroots empowerment, activism, people-to-people, social justice, and citizen exchange projects. Only a few foundations give money to media projects and to peace education in the schools.

The Hewlett Foundation has a program providing long-term institution-building support for academic and practitioner centers that are developing the theory and practice of conflict resolution. A few foundations, such as Winston and McKnight, also fund hands-on conflict resolution activities. Quasi-governmental organizations, such as the U.S. Institute of Peace, the National Endowment for Democracy, and the National Democratic Institute, also provide funds for a variety of activities.

Issues in the Field

The funding process tends to be a cumbersome one, especially in the major foundations. The rigidity of bureaucratic structures makes flexibility and innovation difficult. In addition, bureaucracies prefer tradition and are not eager to change; for example, foundations have been funding security studies for forty years. The world is changing, however, so foundations are finding themselves bound by old priorities and procedures that do not necessarily make sense given the current global scene. Although many are now restructuring their programs and reexamining trends and priorities, that process can take so long that they are always a little out of date and behind the curve.

Another issue has to do with the fact that the time from the inception of an idea to the actual funding of a project can be as much as a year. This makes the pursuit of timely matters challenging and dampens spontaneity. It is extremely difficult for people in the Multi-Track Diplomacy field, which changes as world circumstances change, to know what will be relevant and what they want to be working on a year or more in the future.

Other factors tend to discourage creativity as well. Many foundations give continuously to the same institutions, to those with top names in the field. Individuals, newcomers, new programs, and new institutions find it hard to break into the system. This is especially difficult given the nature of the job scene, where more and more people are creating their own jobs, starting new programs and organizations. Finding the funding to start new institutions when the funding community requires a track record, prefers tried-and-true relationships, and doesn't generally like to fund operational overhead is a major hindrance to creative growth in the field. At the same time, foundations claim that they want to see new faces. Often, however, this means new faces in the same institutions or types of institutions.

A major problem faced by would-be grantees is that funders are usually looking for a measurable result within a specific time frame and a tangible, durable product. Projects that explore processes, that address how rather than what, do not easily meet those criteria. This presents particular hindrances to a field whose leading edge is the exploration of new kinds of processes to prevent and resolve conflicts, for which it is often impossible to prove or evaluate concrete results.

Another constraint on the funding process is that grantees are likely to slant their project proposals toward what they think the funding source is looking for. This can distort the creative process significantly and, over time, lead to a dearth of new thinking. Finally, the inevitable culture bias and worldview of the funders are bound to have an effect on their funding priorities.

Institutions of all sizes in the Multi-Track Diplomacy system are finding that an extraordinary amount of staff time goes to keeping their projects funded. Few organizations can afford to have a full-time grants developer on staff. Small organizations are the most hard hit by this; they have to use their limited research or practitioner personnel to do the extensive work required for writing grant proposals. In most cases, the full range of available grants is never ascertained by grant seekers, simply because they don't have the time and resources to do the exploratory work and the relationship building required to develop wide-ranging options for funding. In addition, some are put off from applying for grants because they are afraid of the process and never push themselves beyond that fear.

The funding community faces some internal communication challenges. Although there is some sharing of information among foundations, there is no systematic communication within the whole system. Especially missing are those links between the mainstream and progressive funders and between foundations and individual philanthropists.

Of increasing concern to the philanthropic community is how to evaluate its projects, especially those involving "soft" processes of dialogue or conflict resolution. Boards like to know that their money has been well spent and has produced specific results, yet the benefits of these types of processes may take many years to come to fruition and then may be traceable to a variety of factors. Some sectors of the multi-track system do not have a history of or an internal culture for evaluating their own activities; others are actively exploring qualitative as well as quantitative methods that might be employed to demonstrate effectiveness. Still others are pioneering the use of creative participatory evaluation modes, in which the evaluation process itself is part of the intervention.

Despite these challenges, the funding community supports a wide range of projects covering those issues and processes that are important to the whole Multi-Track Diplomacy community. There will always be a greater demand and need for money than the funding community, as we know it, will ever be able to meet, in spite of its best intentions. New sources of funding, through the business community, funding networks, and international sources, will simply have to be found to keep up with this fast-growing field.

Place in the Field

The funding world is the financial battery of the system. Without it, much of the activity in the system could not take place. Track Eight occupies a place of great power in the system because of its essential role and because it is the agenda setter and gatekeeper for who does what in the field.

The negative side of this track is the possibility of manipulating that power for ideological or other reasons, as well as the resistance to change built into some of its bureaucratic structures. The positive aspect is the enormous potential for good set in motion by the projects that exist through the generosity of those who give of their resources to make a better world. Another positive aspect is that the wealth that underlies the funding world was, in some cases, accrued through business practices that exploited people and degraded the environment. As that money goes back into the human family to bring peace, a transformational cycle is completed.

Resources

Arca Foundation
1425 Twenty-first St., NW
Washington, DC 20036

(202) 822-9193
Janet Shenk, executive director
This foundation gives grants to groups committed to helping citizens shape public policy, in whatever field.

Robert Barton, President
Catalyst Group
139 Main St.
Brattleboro, VT 05301
(802) 254-8144
Through his work assisting socially responsible business development, Barton connects with a wide range of individual and corporate philanthropists.

Benton Foundation
1634 I St., NW
Washington, DC 20006
(202) 638-5770
This foundation is committed to enhancing the democratic process through public understanding and use of communications and information resources.

Carnegie Corporation of New York
437 Madison Ave.
New York, NY 10022
(212) 371-3200
The Carnegie Corporation gives large grants to universities and institutions with a multidisciplinary approach to issues of security, arms control, and conflict resolution and peace.

Compton Foundation, Inc.
545 Middlefield Rd.
Suite 178
Menlo Park, CA 94025
(415) 328-0101
This foundation gives project grants, general support, and discretionary grants. It is concerned with the prevention of a nuclear holocaust and the amelioration of world conditions that tend to cause conflict and war.

Council on Foundations
1828 L St., NW

Washington, DC 20036-5168
(202) 466-6512
This is a membership organization of grant makers; it provides services to the foundation community, including publications, an annual conference, and technical assistance.

Ford Foundation
320 E. Forty-third St.
New York, NY 10017
(212) 573-5000
The Ford Foundation gives grants for research, training, the development of networks of analysts, and public information on international economics and development; peace, security, and arms control; international refugees and migration; U.S. foreign policy; international relations; international organizations and law; and neglected fields of foreign area studies.

Fund for Peace
1511 K St., NW
Suite 643
Washington, DC 20005
T: (202) 783-4130   F: (202) 783-4767
The fund was established to encourage research and public education on a broad range of issues relating to peace and human rights, covering such topics as arms control, security issues, ethnic relationships, and Third World political, economic, and social development.

General Service Foundation
1445 Pearle St.
Suite 201
PO Box 4659
Boulder, CO 80302
(303) 442-7747
This foundation provides funding for projects in international peace, population, and resources.

William and Flora Hewlett Foundation
525 Middlefield Rd.
Suite 200
Menlo Park, CA 94025-3495

(415) 329-1070
Contact: Steve Toben
The Hewlett Foundation funds organizations that develop conflict resolution theory and practice. It trains and educates people about conflict resolution techniques.

W. Alton Jones Foundation
232 E. High St.
Charlottesville, VA 22902
(804) 295-2134
The Jones Foundation provides grants in two programs: the Sustainable Society Program, which seeks to keep the earth suitable for long-term habitation by preserving the natural resource base; and the Secure Society Program, which seeks to help prevent nuclear war.

John D. and Catherine T. MacArthur Foundation
Program in Peace and International Cooperation
140 S. Dearborn St.
Chicago, IL 60603
(312) 726-8000
The MacArthur Foundation encourages the exploration of peace and cooperation issues in the context of economic, technological, ecological, and political change. It also gives individual research and writing grants and, working with the Social Service Research Council, gives fellowships in peace and security in a changing world.

McKnight Foundation
TCF Tower
121 S. Eighth St.
Suite 600
Minneapolis, MN 55402
(612) 333-4220
The McKnight Foundation's primary interest is in assisting the poor and disadvantaged by enhancing their capacity for productive living. It seeks to strengthen communites and community institutions.

Charles Stewart Mott Foundation
1200 Mott Foundation Building
Flint, MI 48502-1851
(313) 238-5651

The Mott Foundation provides grants in civil society programs and believes that "learning how people can live together most effectively is one of the fundamental needs of humanity."

A. J. Muste Memorial Institute
339 Lafayette St.
New York, NY 10012
(212) 533-4335
The institute sponsors projects that promote the principles and practice of nonviolent social change, peace and disarmament, social and economic justice, racial and sexual equality, and the labor movement.

Peace Development Fund
44 North Prospect St.
PO Box 1280
Amherst, MA 01004
(413) 256-8306
The fund supports local peace and social justice activities throughout the United States to help end the violence that arises from militarism, racism, and economic injustice.

Pew Charitable Trusts
One Commerce Square
Philadelphia, PA 19103-7017
(215) 575-4725
Pew's public policy program supports the development of free markets linked to free political institutions and better understanding of the requirements for maintaining international peace and security in a rapidly changing world.

Ploughshares Fund
Fort Mason Center
San Francisco, CA 94123
(415) 775-2244
Sally Lilienthal, president
The fund seeks to build global security in the nuclear age through the elimination of weapons of destruction and through international cooperation and public debate.

Rockefeller Foundation
420 Fifth Ave.

New York, NY 10018
(212) 869-8500
The Rockefeller Foundation is interested in the nonproliferation of weapons of mass destruction and the redefinition of regional security. It puts less focus on research and more on action. It is creating Arms Watch, a new organization to monitor weapons proliferation and feed that information to the world press.

Threshold Foundation
1388 Sutter St.
Suite 1010
San Francisco, CA 94109
(415) 771-4308
Drummond Pike, director
This is a network of donors with a dual focus—to fund new and unproven ideas while training and activating donor members toward better giving. It funds projects in arts and media, human rights and development, peace, individual and community transformation, and environmental action.

Tides Foundation
1388 Sutter St.
Suite 1010
San Francisco, CA 94109
(415) 771-4308
The Tides Foundation seeks to promote creative nonprofit philanthropic activity and to link diverse individuals seeking social justice, new approaches to economic enterprise, and an enlightened stewardship of our natural environment.

United States Institute of Peace
1550 M St., NW
Washington, DC 20005
(202) 457-1700
Richard Solomon, president
The institute provides solicited (special topic) and unsolicited (general topic) grants in research, education, and training, and it disseminates information on a broad range of issues in peace and conflict resolution. It also offers the Jennings Randolph Fellowship Program, with awards for distinguished fellows, peace fellows, and peace scholars.

Winston Foundation for World Peace
2040 S St., NW
Suite 201
Washington, DC 20009-1110
(202) 483-4215
Contact: Tara Magner
The Winston Foundation focuses on the prevention of nuclear war, broadly understood. It published the *Annual Review of Peace Activism*, a collection of articles on peace education, the news media, citizen diplomacy, and other topics, and publishes the quarterly magazine *Nuclear Times*. It also provides services to the philanthropic community.

Working Assets Funding Service
230 California St.
San Francisco, CA 94111-9876
(415) 788-0777
This service provides "tools for practical idealists," including a Working Assets VISA card and long-distance telephone and travel services. A portion of the money from the fees for these services goes to progressive nonprofit groups working for peace, human rights, the environment, and economic justice.

Track Nine: Communications and the Media
Peacemaking through Information

The primary task of the communications field is to use print, visual, and electronic media to inform and engage the public on issues relating to peace, conflict resolution, and international relations. The basic assumptions of this work are that informed people make good choices and that the media offer an appropriate and necessary forum for public debate and involvement on key issues of global importance.

The media shape public opinion by the information they make available and in turn are a vehicle by which public opinion gets aired. Decision makers, especially in the government, are finely tuned to public opinion as expressed through the media, and their decisions are affected by what they see, hear, and read through the communications channels of this subsystem.

Likewise, modern communications technology enables widespread access to information and opinion sharing, which has tremendous potential for changing how decisions are made and how large groups of people act.

Shape of the Field

We considered three basic categories in the communications field: news reporting, educational media, and electronic communications media.

The first category consists of newspaper, magazine, radio, and television news coverage. By news coverage we mean news reporting and analysis, feature stories and editorial comment, and Cable News Network (CNN). This category also includes some organizations that analyze and monitor news coverage and its relevance to public policy and opinion.

As in some of the other tracks, in addition to the mainstream news media there are budding alternative media. As the technology becomes cheaper, more available, and more user-friendly, the progressive community in particular is using television, film, video, audio, and print media to bring a different view of world events to its constituencies and to the general public.

Educational media, the second category, includes the many types of educational materials produced by countless organizations throughout the Multi-Track Diplomacy system: educational videos, films, radio shows, study guides, and so forth. It also includes the vast array of books, journals, and articles produced from within the system to inform and communicate with other parts of the system: textbooks on peace studies, professional journals, and organizational newsletters, among others.

The third category, electronic communications media, refers to those national and international computer networks that link people throughout the United States and around the globe for conferences and information sharing on topics of interest (particularly the Internet). It also includes space bridges—the use of satellite or digital electronic technology to bring people from different nations and cultures together visually for discussion and sharing.

Culture

The mainstream media are owned and operated by upper-class white males. In the print and television sectors, the system is highly exclusive, fiercely competitive, and driven by economic concerns. Since it relies on both its advertisers, for money, and the government, for access, it tends to be conservative and unwilling to take up issues that are controversial or highly innovative. The progressive media community is more relaxed, less competitive, more adventuresome.

The educational media segment of this field cuts across track boundaries within the multi-track system. Virtually every track produces some kind of educational material for public education and communication. Therefore its culture is as diverse as the many facets of the system.

The electronic communications field, as it relates to peace-building issues, arose mostly out of the citizen diplomacy community and operates from those values and within that culture.

One thing that is true for all these activities, however, is that communication—be it through print, television, satellite, radio, or computer—requires specialized technology and costs money. Therefore, this track is one in which access to money is essential and may determinc not only who participates in the packaging of information but also who receives it. Although television sets are household items in the United States, computers, fax machines, and access to cable channels are not, nor are these media as generally available in other places around the world.

The values of the communications world differ within its subsystems. There is, however, a common belief that although complete objectivity in reporting is not possible, fairness is. There is also a strong belief that fullness of coverage and truth are important and that good information makes the world a better place.

Activities

The activities of the news media involve a vast network of reporters, technicians, and production specialists who are covering world events and trying to make sense of them for the public. Regular news shows account for only a small part of the significant activity in this realm. News commentary in the form of talk shows, roundtables, and analysis shows allows experts from other tracks—especially the government, think tanks, and academia—to comment on and put in perspective the events of the day. These events have the effect of amplifying the voices and the viewpoints of those tracks. Stations do not generally give equal time to activists, the religious community, or citizen diplomats. The same can be said about the opinion and editorial sections of major newspapers. Thus the public debate is framed in ways that perpetrate some of the divisions within the multi-track system and highlight only a portion of the whole system's outlook.

On rare occasions, the major broadcast systems produce in-house documentaries or town meeting or analysis pieces that attempt to look deeply into the complexities of a particular conflict or issue of global peace. Independent filmmakers are doing the same but have great difficulty getting funding and access to the public. For every such show that appears on television there are probably ten that never find their way to the major channels. These use a more private system of distribution through catalogues, libraries, and local showings.

The process is similar in print journalism. Occasionally a senior reporter from one of the major newspapers writes a book about his or her experience in and perception of some conflict area. Independent journalists, not having the same resources available, have a much harder time being published.

VCRs have become a major medium for educational efforts. Videos are highly versatile and easily used by both the public and the schools, and more and more organizations in the Multi-Track Diplomacy community are turning to them to get their message out. Coming out of the Track Two world, the Search for Common Ground Productions' series of ten half-hour shows on applying a conflict resolution process to different topics was probably the most publicly successful of these attempts. The series played on national Public Broadcasting Service (PBS) and cable stations across the country. Other such videos are more likely to be seen by the limited constituency of the organization producing them.

Another product that is plentiful within the system is the professional journal or in-house newsletter. With the recent advent of desktop publishing, virtually any small organization with access to a computer can come up with a simple and attractive layout and design for a publication. The newsletter is an obvious way to communicate with the constituency or to share information across track lines. Likewise, an increasing number of professional papers are appearing at conferences and in journals for cross-fertilization among tracks.

Books, too, are a big factor within the system. Many publishers now focus on works dealing with international relations, peace studies, area studies, conflict resolution, security studies, and world order issues. Textbooks for the growing numbers of college and university classes are being produced.

We are educating ourselves and one another at a furious rate. To keep up with all the new trends and happenings in the field would now require more time than any one person could manage while still doing his or her own work! In part, the electronic conferencing process has emerged to meet this need. PeaceNet, ConflictNet, and EcoNet (all part of the parent group Institute for Global Communications) are three systems that are used widely by members of the Multi-Track Diplomacy community. Through these systems, people are able to carry on extensive dialogues over time, share immediate news and relevant information, and do tasks together without ever leaving their homes or offices. The increasing accessibility of E-mail over the Internet is rapidly establishing electronic communication as a standard vehicle of information exchange.

Electronic digital systems are fast replacing satellite technology for international television hookups. Fax machines are now critical to international communication in all the tracks. Space bridges were once rare because of the cost and elaborate logistics, but with the availability of state-of-the-art digital (essentially telephone) equipment, they are now almost commonplace. Politicians, citizens, businesspeople, and professionals from all walks of life are now communicating across the planet in their own personalized forums. This strengthens the sense of a "global village" and encourages joint enterprises. Common tasks bring people together.

Issues in the Field

The traditional press has been severely affected by rapid global changes. It operates on the mainstream conceptual framework of international relations, so when the Cold War ended and a new world polity began to emerge, the press was challenged to find and convey the proper cognitive system that would explain world events. Whom to interview and what questions to ask became important issues. Since there is no definitive clarity at the top levels of governance about the new shape of world affairs, the press must live in that ambiguous place of deciding how much to rely on the same old sources and how much to depend on new thinkers. The press takes the chance that it will be perceived as going too far in front of the discussions or, conversely, being too embedded in the familiar. This raises the ultimate question that the press must continually face: how much does it shape world events proactively, and how much does it respond reactively?

Another major issue facing the press is the fact that conflict and violence make news and peace doesn't. News is perceived as what's exciting and different. People living happily together are of no interest to the public. Violence is reportable; nonviolence is boring. Thus the activities of the press end up feeding the societal norm of violence and diminishing the possibility of legitimizing nonviolence and resolving conflict peacefully. An interesting by-product of this is that violence that continues for a long time loses its newness and is not reported. Thus conflicts can go on for twenty years or more and drop out of the public eye, gaining attention only when there is some new development in barbarity or a new effort at peacemaking.

The press has other constraints as well. Covering world events means a lot of travel and hard work for the personnel, and it costs dearly. It is not always easy to get into areas where stories are breaking, and staying there can entail great hardship and require courage. Both television shows and newspapers have only so much space for international reporting, so major stories may be treated superficially or not at all. Editorial judgment determines what is important and what isn't, and this controls the picture of world events seen by the American public—a picture that is often very different from the one seen in other countries, where editors may make other choices.

A major issue for the press is how to deal with the feelings and opinions of those reporting the news. Many reporters are stationed in areas for long periods of time and develop large networks of sources and contacts, many of whom become friends. In the course of their work they get deeply grounded in the various perspectives of a situation and come to know the passions of the people intimately. In the best cases, this understanding can be channeled into the reporting, through background and in-depth features. In the worst cases, the knowledge is lost to the system and the feelings are left unexpressed to fester and wound. In no case, to our knowledge, has that profound understanding been called upon by decision makers in their policy deliberations.

Mention should be made here of the role that CNN plays in this system. CNN is the pioneer in changing the relationship between the press and the international diplomacy community. With bureaus located all over the world and twenty-four-hour reporting, CNN is the major source of international news for many governments. Major government offices around the world are hooked up to the CNN system and even use it to relay messages to other governments by making press announcements through CNN programs. Regular diplomatic channels can be much slower and more cumbersome and less deniable.

During the Persian Gulf War, the public too came to rely on CNN. It set the standard for being where the news was. The public, as a result, has come to expect the press to be everywhere and to show everything, instantly. This is a hard precedent to follow for the other major networks, which are not twenty-four-hour news services. It also makes negotiations by public figures nearly impossible. They end up using thirty-second sound bites to satisfy the needs of the media for a statement, but this is not the route to conflict resolution.

In terms of print journalism, one of the critical issues facing the field is access to the venues of opinion making. The op-ed pages of the major national newspapers—the *Washington Post,* the *New York Times,* the *Los Angeles Times,* and the *Christian Science Monitor*—are generally considered to be widely read by and carry great influence with policymakers. The syndicated columnists and guest columnists who write for those pages constitute one of the most elite and powerful groups in the multi-track system. They, and their counterparts in the television press corps, not only have their words in the public eye regularly but also are invited on the public speaking and talk-show circuits, so they wield even greater influence with special-interest groups and the public. This becomes a self-perpetuating cycle, whereby the same small groups of opinion makers and decision makers go round and round reacting to one another. It is a closed system that desperately needs the fresh perspectives and different views of the Multi-Track Diplomacy field.

The ultimate challenge facing the media is how to use their power appropriately. Whether we are talking about who gets to write a guest editorial, whose documentary gets shown on PBS, whose book or article gets published, or who gets computer equipment and satellite access, the issue is the same: how to make the field more inclusive. Those who control the doors to media communication control its content. They control the framing of the issues, the national debate, the range of options presented, the viewpoints available, even the cultural lens through which all this information is seen. Until these doors are thrown open for greater participation—which is beginning to happen in the progressive community but is still far from happening in the mainstream media—the American public will not be fully informed and will choose its leaders and its path accordingly.

Place in the Field

This track serves the information and communication function of the system. It manages the relationship vertically between the public and the decision makers and horizontally among the various members and participants in the Multi-Track Diplomacy system.

The negative aspect of the communication track is that, because of its power to distort and control the information needed throughout the system, it can be a bottleneck for major change and transformation. The positive aspect is that, as communications technology gets cheaper, people all over the planet come closer to one another and to the issues facing us all. We rehumanize the "enemy," see our common humanity, learn from one another's mistakes and successes, and find that we can work together and circumvent, when necessary, the formal obstacles to cooperation.

Resources

Center for Media and Public Affairs
2100 L St., NW
Suite 300
Washington, DC 20037
(202) 223-2942
John Sheehan, executive director
The center conducts scientific studies of how the media treat social and political issues.

CNN
1 CNN Center
PO Box 105366
Atlanta, GA 30348
(404) 827-1500
Steve Hayworth, public relations
This international news network has twenty-four-hour news programming and impacts decision makers by providing instantaneous communication to over 130 world capitals. It offers "World Report," a daily half-hour show of unedited local news broadcasts from around the world, where local groups can share with the international community the events in their regions from their points of view. CNN also produces special documentary shows on topics of peace and war, such as "Waging Peace," a thirty-part global documentary series.

Common Ground Productions
Search for Common Ground

1601 Connecticut Ave., NW
Suite 200
Washington, DC 20036
(202) 265-4300
John Marks, director
Common Ground creates television programs that offer practical examples of a new way for people with opposing views to address their controversies. It produced a ten-part series aired nationally on public television that examined some of the most contentious issues of public policy and international conflict within a framework of conflict resolution.

Jackson Diehl
Editor of the Foreign News Department
Washington Post
1150 Fifteenth St., NW
Washington, DC 20071
(202) 334-6000
Diehl coordinates eighteen news bureaus to provide foreign news coverage for the *Washington Post,* seeking to provide information that will educate readers to world events and motivate their interest in making the world a better place.

Institute for Global Communications
PeaceNet, ConflictNet, and EcoNet
18 De Boom St.
San Francisco, CA 94107
T: (415) 442-0220   F: (415) 546-1794
This computer communications network helps the peace and social change communities cooperate more efficiently through direct communication and computer conferencing.

Jossey Bass Inc., Publishers
350 Sansome St.
San Francisco, CA 94104
(415) 433-1767
Jossey Bass publishes books on conflict resolution, conflict management, and mediation.

Kumarian Press, Inc.
14 Oakwood Ave.

West Hartford, CT 06119
(860) 233-5875
Kumarian Press publishes books on conflict transformation, international development, and global issues.

Coleman McCarthy
Washington Post
1150 Fifteenth St., NW
Washington, DC 20071
(202) 334-7728
Syndicated in fifty newspapers nationally, McCarthy writes two columns a week advocating pacifist, nonviolent approaches to local, national, and international issues. Through writing and teaching he seeks to decrease suffering in the world.

Research Center of War, Peace, and the News Media
New York University
10 Washington Pl., 4th floor
New York, NY 10003
(212) 998-7960
The center is a leading public policy organization devoted to the coverage of international news issues.

James Rubins
Director of Communications
Public Affairs
U.S. Mission to the United Nations
799 United Nations Plaza
New York, NY 10017
(212) 415-4058
Rubins is responsible for press coverage and public affairs for the U.S. Mission to the UN. He provides outreach to help diplomats understand the United States better and enunciates U.S. policy at the UN.

Sage Publications
2455 Teller Rd.
Thousand Oaks, CA 91320
(805) 499-0721
Sage publishes books and journals on conflict resolution, including *Peace and Change: A Journal of Peace Research* and the *Journal of Conflict Resolution.*

St. Martin's Press
Scholarly and Reference Division
175 Fifth Ave.
New York, NY 10010
(212) 674-5151
St. Martin's publishes books on the cutting edge of theory and practice in the field of conflict resolution.

Westview Press
5500 Central Ave.
Boulder, CO 80301
(303) 444-3541
Westview publishes scholarly works, textbooks, and trade books for the general public, with a strong emphasis on international politics, peace studies, and security studies.

Preparing for a New Millennium
Issues Facing the Multi-Track Diplomacy System

The world is indeed changing, and the Multi-Track Diplomacy community is at the forefront of that change, making sense of it as it happens and activating interventions designed to impact the change process. These world developments are the substantive or content focus of the Multi-Track Diplomacy system. They provide the subjects the system addresses through its myriad activities. In this chapter we look at those external and internal issues that have been identified by the system as constituting the bulk of its present and future agenda.

External Issues

When former President Bush used the phrase "new world order," he drew attention to the fact that the global picture is changing and that we must articulate and actualize a new system of international relations to conform with both what is real in the present and what is needed now and for the future. Many in the Multi-Track Diplomacy system are actively engaged in that definition process.

Many believe that we are on an edge between two worldviews, or two paradigms, as our assumptions are shifting about the nature of global order. As we realize the impact of our planetary interdependence, we discover two simultaneous movements in international activities: we see our unity, and we sec our diversity.

On the one hand, we see a greater need for cooperation and collaboration, for collective mechanisms of discussion, negotiation, decision making, peacemaking, economic development and trade, scientific resource sharing, problem solving, environmental action, arms control, and international law and finance. This direction recognizes the need to transcend individualistic, isolationist thinking, to go beyond the boundaries of the nation-state and national sovereignty and deal with common issues from a larger shared forum. It understands the common plight and potential of all humanity, regardless of our superficial differences.

The expansion and strengthening of the European Union, the new international trade agreements (the North American Free Trade Agreement and the World Trade Organization), and the increase in multilateral conferences on environmental, social, and scientific issues are all examples of this thinking. We know that we need this collective mind-set because increasingly our problems transcend national boundaries. We are starting to realize that we must develop new structures and formats for dealing with situations on our shared planet. In conflict resolution terms, we see that win-lose really means lose-lose and that win-win is the only viable approach in an era when losing can mean the end of life as we know it.

On the other hand, even as the nation-state begins to look outdated as the primary unit of political structure, we find ethnic groups rising up to demand that their own identities be politically recognized. Everywhere we turn, our differences confront us. What we once thought of as single nations (Iraq, the Soviet Union, Yugoslavia, Ethiopia, Sudan, India) turn out to be conglomerations of ethnic, religious, or tribal factions whose actions indicate that they no longer wish to be associated. These groups have, in many cases, been repressed or oppressed by ruling factions and will not stand for it any longer. They demand recognition of their basic identity and are increasingly willing to fight for it.

These two thrusts, toward collectivity or unity and toward individuality or diversity, frame many of the significant issues facing the Multi-Track Diplomacy network today. They form the matrix within which the following issues are played out.

Evolving Political Systems

With the dissolution of the Soviet Union, the breakdown of superpower rivalry as a basis for world order, and the disintegration of communism as a major ideological structure for state power, political systems and relationships are in massive flux. The democratization process is sweeping not just Eastern Europe but also Africa and Central and South America and is now in the forefront of discussions in the Middle East as well. We are discovering that the transition from authoritarianism to democracy is not easy, either politically or economically. These transitions are creating conditions that we have no established means of dealing with, conditions that themselves may be transitory. Our bureaucratic and institutionalized systems of government cannot keep up with these rapid developments.

How do we help countries develop the new economic, political, and social structures they need to complete their democratization processes? How do we understand this process in a general way and support each country in its unique circumstances? How do we work with the economic and environmental devastation and the political chaos undergirding the foundations of many of these nations in transition? How do we deal with the lawless "warlord" or "mafia" phenomenon that frequently arises during times of profound change? How does the increasingly frequent use of citizen empowerment— in the form of massive street demonstrations demanding changes in leadership and policy—become integrated as a tool of political statecraft, and what other tools of statecraft do we need to create? These are some of the questions that face the world community and the Multi-Track Diplomacy community.

Regional and Identity-Group Conflicts

As the superpower dichotomy shifts, so too do the picture and pattern of conflicts around the globe. No longer merely stand-ins or clients for East-West rivalry, nations and peoples are demonstrating their intense and long-overshadowed need for identity, recognition, and inclusion. After focusing for so long on the possible effects of nuclear war between the two superpowers, the world is now witnessing the marginalized, the unheralded, the unrepresented peoples engaging in battle—often long-term, protracted battle—for their rights of self-determination.

Chechens, Croatians, Kurds, Mohawks, Sikhs, Shi'ites, Tamils, Tigrayans, and others are joining Palestinians, Northern Irish Catholics, black South Africans, and others in seeking their place in the world community. These groups are fighting for their identities, not for ideology. Nor do their populations conform to national boundaries. Of the estimated 5,000 peoples and nations in the world, only 185 are represented as nation-states in the United Nations, and of these, 26 are new members that have joined in the last five years. The struggles of these peoples to take their true place in the world community with dignity and with the respect of others for their uniqueness will shape the destiny of the world scene for decades to come.

These conflicts are unlike those imagined in the Cold War era, for which vast quantities of nuclear arms were produced as a deterrent. These conflicts are regional or subregional in nature, or intrastate rather than international, and they often involve peoples and cultures about which we know very little, who have not played major roles in our international scenarios to date. In addition, the long unmet needs of repressed groups, or of groups that believe that their unique identities are threatened by the movement toward collectivism and unity, are increasingly being expressed through fanaticism and terrorism.

We are also discovering that the long-term effects of these conflicts take us to the very edge of or beyond our present capacity to deal with the psychological factors of large groups. Cycles of violence that beget more violence, repression that produces aggressive reactions, also engender deep issues that we barely know how to deal with in our individual lives, let alone in a global setting. How will the Rwandan people come to terms with their loss? How will the refugees and rape victims of the wars in the former Yugoslavia ever heal their profound wounds? How will younger generations of Palestinians and Israelis ever forgive one another for the mutual hurt? How will the tortured and the families of the disappeared in Argentina, Chile, and El Salvador ever be reconciled with their oppressors? How will those who have abused power at the expense of others ever acknowledge their wrongs and show contrition?

Changing Views of Power and Violence

As a result of the increased awareness of our global interdependence and of the mass-destruction capability of our high-tech weapons systems, as well as an evolving moral sense, many people around the world are recognizing the need to move away from violence and force as a means of solving problems. This may also be related to the changing nature of our intergroup relations. For too long we have assumed a society based on the notion of power and dominance, that one individual or entity could control and have dominion over another (including the environment and nonhuman life-forms) and, for various reasons, even had the right to do so. This led to a geopolitical system based on relative power, with military might as the ultimate enforcer.

Now we are acknowledging the need for and the reality of partnership, or mutually beneficial cooperation, and power begins to look more like the ability to do something together rather than to wield control over another. This is a major transformation in human experience, and we are in the midst of it—one foot in the past and one in the future. As in any change process, the forces of resistance and fear of the unknown become stronger as we get closer to new and perhaps healthier ways of being. But so too do the forces for change.

As the worldview shifts and we begin to see our relatedness, it becomes harder to aim weapons at those who are part of our global family. As we confront the painful and deeply embedded consequences of those systems of dominance that have changed in our recent past (slavery, imperialism, colonialism) and the brutal and dehumanizing effects of those that are still actively embraced in many parts of the world (sexism, racism, totalitarianism, authoritarianism, torture), some of us become less inclined to continue to use force. After witnessing the devastation we have created and can create through our advanced weapon systems, many are seeking another way.

In this context, arms control in the Middle East, a subject unthinkable until recently, is now on the table. U.S. spending for defense is being reviewed, and the conversion of the defense industry to non-defense-related manufacturing is becoming a major endeavor in the business community.

We are beginning to realize that the reason behind our enormous arms buildup—the threat of a land war in Central Europe against the former Soviet Union—is no longer a realistic possibility. Therefore the debate in the United States, at least, is now centered on redefining our national security concerns and the means of addressing them. This debate is wide-ranging and involves an ongoing political discourse about what is in our national interest, the role of the United States as the sole remaining superpower, the importance of the U.S. position in global markets, and our relationship to international alliances and structures.

We are also becoming aware of the profound effects of structural violence within our societies. We recognize the legacy of prolonged economic and social injustice—where our very institutions subtly encourage violence toward the poor and the marginalized—and we are beginning to address issues of domestic abuse, substance abuse, homelessness, and crime in different ways. We are realizing that peace at home and abroad is impossible without justice.

Meanwhile, there is a growing and spreading commitment to nonviolence as a means of addressing our differences and solving our problems. The field of conflict resolution is blossoming, especially in our internal social spheres. Mediation and conflict resolution are being taught in the schools and used in the courts, the playgrounds, and the workplace. Large-group methods of nonviolence are also being explored. The world watched in awe as government after government in Eastern Europe toppled as a result of peaceful demonstrations by the people.

Although it may be too early to say that there is an international mass movement to delegitimize war, those currents are in the air. There seems to be a movement toward legitimating conflict resolution and peacemaking as supplemental if not yet alternative tools of international relations.

At the same time, there is an increasing breakdown of order and a failure of the international community to deal effectively with conflicts in which their own national interests are not identified. Conflicts in the former Yugoslavia, Somalia, and Rwanda paint an ominous picture of a world in which outside agents, including the United Nations, are helpless to act to deescalate violence, mediate a settlement, or prevent the spread of conflict. Likewise, the fighting in Sudan, Chechnya, and the Kurdish parts of Turkey and Iraq demonstrate the paralysis of the international community when conflicts are defined as "internal matters."

The bombings of the World Trade Center and the Oklahoma City federal building, the gas attacks on the Japanese subways, and the increased illegal sale of nuclear materials demonstrate that terrorism knows no boundaries and alerts us to the inherent danger of terrorist attacks at any time and from any direction.

Finally, the decline in credibility of the UN and NATO—their inability to hold back the tide of chaos and violence or even to sustain the massive humanitarian needs of war victims, refugees, and displaced populations—suggests that people have little to fear by pursuing violence as a means to achieve their ends.

Globalization of the World Economy

A new era is emerging in international relations in which geopolitics is no longer necessarily the primary focus of relations between governments. Increasingly, issues associated with the global marketplace are coming to the fore as factors that define and impinge on policy decisions. Jobs, trade opportunities, expanding markets, and investment potential are driving the political agendas of major states and determining how they treat one another. The U.S. government's recognition of Vietnam and its complex relations with China indicate that economic concerns may be overshadowing ideological and human rights issues in determining policies. The U.S.-Japan standoff on market access indicates that trade wars may become an all-too-familiar scenario in the near future.

Environmental Sustainability

Many in the Multi-Track Diplomacy community see averting environmental disaster as the greatest challenge of our times. We are increasingly aware of the fragility of our ecosystems and the dangerous levels of degradation and depletion we have brought upon ourselves. The sustainability of the earth as a life-support system is in doubt. The burning of the oil fields in Kuwait is a reminder that our tools for environmental self-destruction are no longer separate from our political lives.

Growing environmental consciousness has been finding multiple expressions in the political arena. We are challenged at every level of governance to find creative solutions to environmental problems. This constitutes one of the greatest topics of multilateral discussions among nations, since all environmental problems are global and can be solved only through multilateral interaction. New professional fields and competencies are arising to deal with the negotiation and cross-cultural communication processes that must be used to address these issues at a planetary level and to understand the scope of the problems. Science and politics, business and peacemaking are being tied together in new and unfamiliar ways.

Environmental depletion, as well as man-made environmental catastrophe, is fast becoming a major threat to world security. As fossil fuel and water supplies are being depleted, competition for scarce resources becomes a major factor in international relations. The potential for violent conflict over water, oil, or minerals is a specter that humanity must face in the coming decades.

Multi-Track Diplomacy's Role

The aforementioned concerns have become the content of the research, education, and action modes of the Multi-Track Diplomacy system. This represents a recent shift in the shape and direction of the system's activities.

Until recently, much of the attention of the peacemaking community was focused on issues of nuclear war, security, and arms control in the context of U.S.-Soviet relations. For two generations the Cold War provided the primary context for political, economic, and diplomatic thinking. Peace was thought of primarily in terms of superpower relations. Research funding was focused on security studies; grassroots organizations concentrated on antinuclear activities. Think tanks looked endlessly at Cold War issues—some even came into being during the Reagan years to bring the conservative anticommunist perspective to the intellectual and programmatic arenas.

Citizen diplomacy became a significant movement in the 1980s through the burgeoning numbers of Americans who went to the Soviet Union and gained firsthand experience of the "enemy" as human and personable. Supplemental diplomacy, the Dartmouth and the Pugwash Conferences, were geared toward dialogue between U.S. and Soviet counterparts. The most visible example of business diplomacy for a long time was Armand Hammer's dealings with the Soviet Union.

The religious community and the international development community were exceptions to this focus on U.S.-Soviet relations. They have traditionally been more attentive to the Third World and its unique issues apart from any Cold War implications.

In the last several years, the predominant focus has shifted dramatically. It has happened so fast, in fact, that some institutions are playing catch-up, as they retool their structures to meet the new world realities. This is especially so of the foundation world, which has found itself challenged by habitual thinking and procedures as it seeks to address new topics. Now there is an explosion of interest in the concerns implicit in the rapidly changing world order.

Where there was once an interest in security studies, attention is now given to nation building. Those in the academic, research, business, and practitioner communities who were involved in U.S.-Soviet relations are now active in the new nations of Eastern Europe and Central Asia, working at every level to build structures of governance, economy, and social services. Training programs in conflict resolution skills are being offered in these regions, and conflict resolution centers and peace institutes are being set up in many countries.

With the attention turning away from superpower proxy conflicts, much of the field is now concerned with identity-group conflict and with the regional ethnic, tribal, religious, and factional fighting that is rampant throughout the world. As diplomats, academics, and researchers look to the political ramifications, the business community extends into new markets and begins to see an expanded role for itself in peace building. In the educational community, the fields of global education and cross-cultural studies have greatly expanded.

The religious community and private voluntary organizations, which have always been active in the developing world, are becoming not only more visible to the rest of the system but also more active behind the scenes. The activist community is extending itself into the causes of less visible peoples such as the Tibetans and Afghans. Citizen exchange programs are sending greater numbers to Central America, the Middle East, and Eastern Europe.

In the conflict resolution community, there continues to be a focus on long-term protracted conflicts and, more recently, on those that have not been center stage in the world's attention. Part of the growth in this field is the increase in attention to psychological issues of large-group healing and reconciliation. This is bringing increasing numbers of psychiatrists, psychologists, and other health and healing professionals into the network.

As regions become more open to outside help, an extensive debate is surfacing among conflict resolution theorists and practitioners concerning the proper ethics, methodologies, and assumptions of third-party intervention. Theoretical frameworks that deal with analyzing, managing, and resolving conflicts are being devised and refined in academic and practitioner centers around the United States. New bodies of literature are beginning to appear about needs-based versus interest-based conflict analysis, about elicitive versus prescriptive approaches, about single-text negotiation versus problem-solving formats. We are starting to look at families and family therapy in relation to the world family and its need for help. Much study and discussion are occurring about the nature of identity-group conflicts. Many have realized that within our own borders we have ongoing identity-group conflicts, and they too provide an important basis for learning.

Another response of the conflict resolution community is to set up regional and international centers for conflict resolution. The Carter Center's International Negotiation Network has taken the lead in this field, but several people are working with groups in Europe and Africa to build regional centers and networks of skilled individuals who can be called on to mediate, train, and consult with parties in conflict. American experts are becoming catalysts for people in other nations who want to build institutions that can deal with the conflict in their lives.

Certain topics that were once considered "far out" are now mainstream. For instance, ten years ago, the issue of economic conversion involved a few activists pitted against major corporations. Now small and large businesses are voluntarily converting away from defense production, and a network and support system of people working on the issue have developed. Terrorism—once a subject that was addressed only by State Department officials who had to deal with hijackings and hostages—is now a subject for Track Two and Track One discussions within and between numerous nations. Those studying social movements now have the whole phenomenon of mass citizen demonstrations to analyze, as do those involved in nonviolence studies.

The religious community has taken a more visible role in issues of war and peace, as witnessed during the war in the Persian Gulf, where it was not just the traditional peace churches that spoke out and sent delegations to the gulf but also the mainstream churches. The media, too, in being present at events as they happen, have taken a more active role in analyzing world affairs, in some cases in controversial ways. In the past few years, we have witnessed groundbreaking television programs on issues that were previously considered too delicate or too complex to discuss, such as Ted Koppel's town meetings or documentary films on the Palestinians. During the Gulf War, CNN's presence in Baghdad was electrifying.

Satellite technology has allowed space bridges to provide instantaneous links between citizens and policymakers in different countries for mutual discussion. It has also been a major innovation within the citizen diplomacy community. That same technology now brings heads of state or key foreign spokespeople directly into American living rooms on regular nightly broadcasts.

The environmental situation has had a major impact on the Multi-Track Diplomacy community. Environmental issues have essentially been brought into the field at every level, so that the traditional ideas of peace with justice, peace with freedom, peace with development, and peace with security now include, as a matter of course in the minds of many, peace with environmental integrity.

The Multi-Track Diplomacy system is also responding to these issues in more general ways. It is seeking to define its terms more precisely, considering what peace, peacemaking, and peacebuilding really are. It is also looking at the entire change agent process, considering how we make changes of a significant nature in large social systems and what qualities, moral standards, training, and expertise such change agents should have.

The system is examining the telescoping nature of peaceful systems as well. It is giving attention to the need to work for peace and with conflict at every level of human behavior, from the individual through the family, the neighborhood, the community, the workplace, and the world. Theoreticians and practitioners are looking particularly at the relationship between domestic and international conflict: what qualities and characteristics hold true at all levels, and what translation of methodologies can we make between one and another?

While we are looking at the external issues that are currently engaging the attention of the Multi-Track Diplomacy community, it is also useful to mention some issues that are not being examined. Much of the international focus is still on Europe, the former Soviet Union, and the Middle East, and less attention is being paid in the Multi-Track Diplomacy system to the Caribbean, Latin America, and Africa.

By and large, the major overwhelming economic, social, and political problems and the serious armed conflicts throughout Africa are not foremost on the system's agenda. Likewise, we see little research, education, or action in such "hot" areas as Cambodia, North and South Korea, Burma, India, and Pakistan or with the indigenous peoples of North and South America.

However, now that South Africa, El Salvador, Northern Ireland, and the Middle East are in various stages of peaceful transitions, we are witnessing the rise of comparison studies in which researchers, practitioners, and activists are looking to the successes to extract and transfer learning that might apply in other, still largely intractable, situations.

Internal Issues

As the Multi-Track Diplomacy system addresses the external issues of the world, it is also dealing with its own internal processes. In this section we examine those systemic issues, issues that have less to do with the content of conflict than with the process of how we manage our relationships and define our field.

Taking a Systemic Overview

One of the key issues facing the Multi-Track Diplomacy system is that it does not yet think of itself as a system. Although there are certain natural alliances among the nine tracks (for instance, between academia and conflict resolution, the government and think tanks, religious and activist groups, or funding and research), few of the players think of the whole system or consider themselves to be part of any larger whole. In fact, the tendency is to be insular, to believe that each particular way is the only way—the most significant path—and that other directions and dimensions, if they exist, are of less importance.

This means that all the information, wisdom, skill, and resources of the system are not freely shared among all parts of the whole. People are making decisions and taking action without the benefit of all the available resources. There are overlaps and gaps within the whole, and there is competition and distrust between groups that could benefit greatly from cooperation. It also means that people are not aware of the existence of some of their peers and colleagues from whom, given their different perspectives, they could learn a great deal.

Since there are no major institutions that see the system as a whole and whose job it is to service the whole, these gaps go unfilled and often unnoticed. Few individuals and institutions are doing leadership development or cross-track training or systematically addressing the issues that impact the whole system. No one is a true spokesperson for the field, and no one is the catalyst, vision holder, or standard-bearer.

Legitimizing the Field

The very field and process of peacemaking have yet to be fully legitimized in American society. Whether this is a cause or a result of the lack of systemic thinking, it is evident in various ways.

Peace studies and conflict resolution programs throughout the academic community are struggling to be accepted as serious disciplines and to become institutionalized within the fabric and structure of their universities. Although several hundred such programs now exist, few exist as departments in and of themselves; they tend to be multidisciplinary programs or subspecialties within a regular department. Only a handful of universities give master's or Ph.D. degrees specifically called peace studies or conflict resolution.

Many of these academic programs receive outside funding that allows them to get started, but that funding often comes with the expectation that the college or university will eventually incorporate the program into its budget. The schools, many of which are facing financial problems themselves, do not have the resources to take over the funding of these programs, even though there may be many students involved. In several institutions of higher learning, dedicated professors teach courses in peace studies without pay.

The issue of legitimacy is a major one in the interface between the government and the professional conflict resolution community. In some government circles, negotiation is still assumed to mean compromise and to be a sign of weakness. Only one conflict resolution specialist that we know of was called in to advise high-level policymakers about the Persian Gulf crisis. Former President Jimmy Carter's efforts at peacemaking in various "hot spots" are often treated with some degree of scorn by other politicians and the press. Such private initiatives are still seen by most officials as either immaterial or detrimental to the "real" process of diplomacy.

Given that view, it is difficult for the growing body of conflict resolution theory and practice to take what it sees as its rightful place in the political process. It also raises the question of how policymakers and the public can be educated to a clearer understanding of what conflict resolution can achieve, and how it can be incorporated into existing procedures. Again, because there is no institution viewing the whole, this education process is left in the hands of individuals who feel some need to act. This is one of those issues that people frequently shake their heads about but don't define as their responsibility.

Even within the conflict resolution field, legitimacy is a key concern. How people who wish to be included in that community are judged still rests with traditional tests of academic achievement (Ph.D.) and affiliation (what organizations or individuals one works with or for). "Who did you study with" is a question that is often asked, and individuals who seek entry in ways other than the accepted channels find themselves isolated.

Other fields within the nine tracks also struggle with the credibility issue. The religious community is easily written off by decision makers and others as lightweight, yet it probably has the most extensive networks on the ground in conflict areas. It has the best track record of successful behind-the-scenes intervention and the clearest vision of what is just and what is possible. The activist community is routinely delegitimated by policymakers, yet it too has an important viewpoint, significant skills in grassroots organizing, and a profound awareness of the human aspects of policy issues.

Citizen diplomacy is frequently seen as "interesting" but not important, and it is often viewed by Track One as a nuisance or even as detrimental to the work of "real" diplomats. Business is just beginning to be acknowledged as having an important role in the peacemaking process, whereas the media and funding communities are sometimes seen as outside the process altogether.

Peace institutes, too, are struggling to be fully accepted. It took many years and much controversy for Congress and the executive branch to arrive at the creation of the U.S. Institute of Peace. Now that it is in place, policy officials who could benefit from its findings do not necessarily seek it out as a resource. Ambassador Samuel Lewis, then president of the U.S. Institute of Peace and doorway to its collective wisdom, would have been a logical place for the Bush administration to start on August 2, 1990, in exploring conflict resolution possibilities in the gulf. But Lewis was not asked to advise the president or his immediate circle.

The Iowa Peace Institute, which is the model of state and citizen-sponsored peace institutes, and whose structure and process are being emulated in several states seeking to develop like institutions, is struggling to maintain its legitimacy. Even though it has demonstrated years of successful action and service to Iowa and the world, the Iowa legislature is divided over the value of providing one-third of the institute's funding from state resources.

Until all these functions are legitimated, until all these groups acknowledge one another's vital role, and until peace and peacemaking are valued by the leaders and the public, this field will continue to operate at far less than its full potential.

Professional Development

Along with issues of legitimacy come concerns about professional growth. As more and more private citizens include themselves in peacemaking processes in various ways, issues of training, standards, and ethics arise.

Each of the nine tracks of the Multi-Track Diplomacy community has basically been dealing with these items internally. That is, whatever training programs, professional standards, or ethical guidelines exist do so within each field; there is no overall coordination or even communication. Thus the skills and behaviors of religious or development practitioners, for instance, as they work behind the scenes to help resolve conflicts, may be totally different from those of academic professionals or of politically appointed or career diplomats. Then too, within each field, the resources for training and the consideration of professional standards and ethics are often sparse or nonexistent.

The diplomatic community is responsible for negotiating innumerable treaties and agreements among nations. The State Department sends out a thousand official delegations a year to international multilateral conferences. Yet very few diplomats receive more than token training in bilateral or multilateral negotiating skills. This lack is so apparent that the Academy of American Diplomacy, a group of retired diplomats, joined with the School of Advanced International Studies at Johns Hopkins University to create a project on multilateral negotiation that examined case studies and described the multilateral negotiation process in ways that are useful to theoreticians and practitioners.

Training for Track Two professionals is also haphazard. George Mason University now offers a Ph.D. program in conflict analysis and resolution. Harvard's project on negotiations, Syracuse's program on the analysis and resolution of conflicts, American University's master's program in peace and conflict resolution, and Eastern Mennonite University's program on conflict analysis and transformation are in place; other universities offer programs in negotiation, mediation, and conflict resolution skills. Nonuniversity training programs are offered by CDR in Colorado and the Institute for Multi-Track Diplomacy in Washington, D.C. No unified or even coordinated curricula exist, nor are there any standardized criteria for what constitutes professional practictioner ability.

The range of practitioners in the field, at least among the older generation, reflects a wide spectrum of background, experience, and methodology. Some come from the world of official diplomacy, some from the law or higher education; some are academicians and others psychologists or psychiatrists; some have a mediation background in public policy, labor relations, or family disputes, and others come by way of involvement in social movements.

The next generation of conflict resolution specialists seems to be coming through the academic door. They are taking their advanced degrees at such places as Harvard, Syracuse, American, Eastern Mennonite, or George Mason and are training under key practitioners associated with their institutions. Thus we are starting to see schools of practice developing. With hundreds of potential peacemakers in the academic pipeline in undergraduate and graduate programs, it will be interesting to see how the field develops in the future.

Activists, private citizens, religious and international development workers, businesspeople, and journalists get whatever training they receive from their particular peer groups or from their experiences in the field.

Except for Track One, then, where individuals are hired and assigned to specific tasks with some sense of accountability, the whole unofficial field of peacemaking is somewhat haphazard in terms of accountability. A "Guide for Newcomers to Track Two Diplomacy," first suggested by Kathleen Kennedy and written by John McDonald, does exist, but the field is without uniform guidelines of professional or ethical behavior.[1] Whether this constitutes a problem is beginning to be discussed in various forums. In this situation, if the groups would just talk with one another, they could learn the different ways that these issues are being addressed. This could prevent the "reinventing the wheel" syndrome and could lead to greater consistency.

These are important issues, because nonofficial interventions in conflicts can create counterproductive conditions as far as governments are concerned. Also, inept intervention can make already fragile situations much worse. These are life-and-death circumstances, not for the peacemakers so much as for the combatants. How change agents come into, interact with, and leave conflict systems can create unintended effects that may have a great impact, both positive and negative. Therefore, who operates in these roles and what can reasonably be expected of them in terms of training and sensitivity is a critical issue.

Some of the ethical questions that have arisen in the field are as follows: Who are we to intervene? What is our personal agenda? How well trained are we in our appropriate technologies and methodologies? How much do we know about the conflict, the people, and culture we are stepping into? How much should we know? Under what circumstances should we be neutral process observers or partial participants? How do we avoid overlaying our own cultural assumptions on others? How sensitive are we to cultural differences? How time committed are we? Who will address these questions, individually and on a systemic level?

Diversity

Mirroring the global patterns of unity and diversity, the field has its own identity-group issues. The differences in the field are noticeable in several arenas.

In terms of ethnicity, the Multi-Track Diplomacy system is strikingly Eurocentric and overwhelming white and male. Institutionally empowered women and people of color are still rare. The effect of this uniformity or lack of ethnic and gender diversity is subtle and hard to detect. We believe that it cannot but touch the very heart of the system's task. Most of the conflicts today are in the Third World and involve peoples from cultures that are radically different from ours. They are between people whose ethnic backgrounds are far removed from white European or American experience. How our ethnocentric lens affects the way we influence those conflicts is a topic that has begun to be examined.

Are our models and methodologies inherently flawed by being products of our own culture, or are they truly universal and beyond cultural differences? How does our inevitable ethnocentricity and personal cultural sensitivity affect our work? How is our cultural homogeneity reflected in our theories, our practice? How are we ourselves robbed of the richness that comes with different perspectives? These are important questions to which we have few answers. Many in the field are involved in cross-cultural studies and are addressing these issues, at least in terms of the work in the world.

The gender issue is also important. Although it is the men who do most of the soldiering, women suffer tremendously as a result of war. Men and women have different perspectives on issues of war and peace, violence, and relationships, but we can't fully explain or understand how or why this is so. An article in the *Washington Post* on the differences between men's and women's views on war suggests that in spite of several decades of "liberation," women are still more likely to think of the personal consequences of violence to both sides and address relationship and feeling issues. Men are more likely to think of long-term strategies and technologies and be more black and white in their moral thinking.[2]

Regardless of the details of the differences between ethnic, racial, and gender groups, what matters most is that the system is impoverished and handicapped when it does not carry the fullness of diversity. Sameness of view and assumptions, even at subtle and unconscious levels, engenders complacency and stagnation. Differences stimulate; they inject excitement and the need for creative synthesis. Since these are the very challenges facing our diverse world community, for total congruence, the Multi-Track Diplomacy community should also address these issues.

In our research, we found only two organizations that seriously embodied ethnic and gender diversity: Clergy and Laity Concerned and the NTL Institute of Applied Behavioral Science. Perhaps there are others, but in our interviewing process, these two stood out. Each of these organizations, originally created by white men, underwent a conscious, deliberate, and ongoing process to diversify its membership and leadership. Their experiences and results would make instructive studies for other institutions.

Gender differences are publicly discussed in some of the Multi-Track Diplomacy communities, but there is a long way to go to bring women into the system and have them fully empowered, especially at top levels of decision making. What is happening is that organizations are becoming sensitized to these issues outside themselves, usually by studying cross-cultural concerns regarding the client systems—the people in whose conflicts they are intervening. Turning this awareness inside to our own system will be a major challenge of the next decade.

Diversity issues are also present in the area of age. Young people are not consulted or included as a matter of course in any of the nine tracks, except the academic field. There, they are seen primarily as passive clients of the system, not active cocreators of it. In the conflict resolution community, the generational issue is a particularly acute one, because the younger generation's only access to experience in the field is through the gatekeeping of their elders and teachers.

Representatives of various disciplines are missing in the Multi-Track Diplomacy system. Scientists, economists, applied behavioral scientists, practitioners from the many schools of psychology (especially the humanistic approaches), physicians, nurses and other health care workers, artists, labor officials—these are some of the fields that are not always fully represented in the Multi-Track Diplomacy community, but they have critical expertise. Some have organized and empowered themselves to play a role through citizen diplomacy, such as Physicians for Social Responsibility. Others are simply not thought of or consulted.

Those who traditionally deal with human behavior, such as organizational development specialists and those from the psychological and healing arts, have developed alternative methodologies and analyses of conflict and conflict resolution and are increasingly taking that work out into the world. They are doing so, however, with little coordination and communication with the more mainstream parts of the system. This too is a missed opportunity for resource sharing; this expertise could be incorporated into the whole so that all could benefit.

The same can be said about groups that have studied non-Western philosophies and the martial arts. They have little or no credibility in the Multi-Track Diplomacy community but have a great understanding of human behavior in groups and ways of dealing with it for more harmonious relationships. The Multi-Track Diplomacy community will soon be faced with the need to look in its own backyard.

Other differences exist within the system and are equally important. There are great differences among conceptual frameworks and methodologies for understanding the nature of conflict, peace, and the process of peacemaking. Constructive debates rage among Track One and Track Two practitioners and theorists about a whole range of issues. Should we be developing strategies for managing power politics better, or is the time of power politics over, and should we be addressing identity-group concerns instead? Are international relations about interactions between governments, or about long-term relationships between "whole bodies politic"?[3] Should basic human needs or strategic interests be the focus of our attention? As we address the political side of world affairs, what place do we give to human, economic, and environmental concerns? Can principles of international negotiation be applied both nationally and locally in resolving family and community disputes, and vice versa? Can anyone be trained in negotiation skills, or are we born with, or without, those abilities?

Other questions address conflict resolution modes more directly. Is the role of the conflict facilitator to manage a process that is ultimately about relationship building or to achieve a specific outcome?

Should the facilitator be totally neutral and outside the situation, or is there a role for the insider–partial mediator? What is the legitimate mix between grassroots efforts and outside experts? Can their relationship be consciously planned and coordinated?

When is mediation the proper approach, and when should joint problem solving be used? Should we be attempting to settle conflicts, manage them, ripen them, transform them, or all of these? Can we assume a shared understanding of what these terms mean? What are proper prenegotiation activities, and who should undertake them? What about our cultural differences? These subjects and others are areas in which there are real differences of opinion within the Multi-Track Diplomacy community, but forums for their discussion are limited and insular.

Finally, there are differences within the system among those who consider themselves theoreticians, practitioners, and researchers. There are also differences among those for whom involvement in peacemaking or peacebuilding is an avocation and those for whom it is a career or a life commitment. The tendency is to segregate and band together with like-minded peers.

The challenge is to name, confront, accept, and grow from our differences without having to convert, disempower, control, co-opt, or diminish those who are different from us, and to do so because we know that without all perspectives the circle is not complete, the whole is not fulfilled. This remains the critical issue, whatever the substance of the diversity might be. It is perhaps the greatest challenge of our world today, so it is no surprise that we find it throughout the fabric of the Multi-Track Diplomacy system. In reflection of the world "out there," we find few if any structures or conscious vehicles for dealing effectively with this process.

Resources

Money appears to be the biggest single issue facing the vast majority of the programs, projects, and organizations in the Multi-Track Diplomacy community. Virtually everyone we interviewed cited the lack of money, the difficulty of raising money, or the competing demands for limited funds as a major concern, in many cases *the* major concern. This was true even in the foundation and philanthropic world, where the ups and downs of the economy have, in some cases, led to decreased investment income. It was as true in organizations with large budgets and eminent reputations as in small, unknown institutions.

Most of the activities within the Multi-Track Diplomacy community do not generate income. In fact, in Track Two and elsewhere in the system, much of the work is pro bono. Although individuals may have salaries that cover some or all of their peacemaking activities, the activities themselves produce little or no income. Exceptions to this include business activities that may have peacebuilding as a by-product and some mainstream media, mostly print and television, that gain money from the sale of advertising or books.

This is an important factor in understanding the work of this system, and it may be critical to the field's lack of credibility. Essentially, the Multi-Track Diplomacy system is a service industry in an economic context where production is honored. Its activities do not produce goods and material resources, and its results are often intangible, elusive, subtle, and difficult to evaluate. In this country, the service industry is traditionally paid and valued less than other segments of the economy. Results that can't be touched, sold, reproduced, or even proved are viewed skeptically and held in low esteem. In this regard, people in the Multi-Track Diplomacy community seeking financial resources suffer from the double burden of having to compete for apparently limited funds and having to prove the worth of their work.

How institutions get their money varies widely within the system. Some have dues-paying members but also need special fund-raising appeals to their general constituencies to meet overhead costs and take on special projects. The academic and research communities rely heavily on the foundation world. The grassroots community has its own set of foundations that fund activist projects. Although some of the major foundations are heavily endowed, others depend on contributions from their own individual supporters.

Individual supporters seem to be important across the board— from small donors to huge contributors. Private individuals are increasingly looked to as a means of support for organizations both large and small. It is instructive in this regard to remember the work of Oliver North and other Reagan aides who solicited large sums from wealthy Americans and foreign governments to support aspects of the president's foreign policy agenda. Even the U.S. government looks for wealthy donors.

Many of the groups within the Multi-Track Diplomacy system have their own natural constituencies from which they derive their support and solicit contributions. Religious groups have their congregations. The media have their advertisers. Think tanks and academia have their favorite foundations. Citizen groups have their colleagues of like mind. Activists turn to friendly foundations and special donors in the progressive community.

The one group that seems to fall between the cracks in having a natural constituency, and therefore a source of funding, is the conflict resolution community. The people who benefit from its services are not funding sources, nor can they be asked to pay fees for the services rendered. There is no natural appeal to the public to form any kind of membership basis of support, nor are foundations happy about funding activities whose end results are so unpredictable and immeasurable. Foundation staffs need to be able to show their boards that their money was spent for activities whose merit can be clearly evaluated and demonstrated. Then too, many conflict resolution practitioners work for institutions that require other forms of work from them—teaching, administrative, research, or other activities— and can devote only limited time to peacemaking work.

The response to this problem has been varied. Several practitioners we spoke with said that they spend inordinate amounts of time trying to raise the money to do the work; as a result, their time and capacity to actually perform the necessary services are greatly diminished. Others, out of frustration and a sense of urgent need, simply pay out of their own pockets to get to where their work is in demand, and many donate their time as well. A few have found one or more individuals to sponsor their work, but except for one independent citizen peacemaker in California who has an ongoing private sponsorship arrangement with a wealthy patron, even this involves a constant process of solicitation and carries the stress of uncertainty.

Another subsystem that falls through the cracks is the filmmaking community. There are many excellent filmmakers who could produce documentaries, series, and all kinds of innovative shows about issues of conflict and peacemaking, but these undertakings are enormously expensive and very difficult to guarantee a market for. This may well be one of the most underutilized parts of the system in terms of educating the public, partly because of the financial difficulties involved.

There are questions about finances that the entire system should be addressing: What creative sources for funding might we pursue? What is the relationship between legitimacy issues and funding? How might we build coalitions and joint undertakings to overcome the tendency to see the grant process as competitive? How might the business community, which has vast resources, be more effectively involved in the funding process? How might the current funding sources—the foundations and philanthropists from both mainstream and alternative perspectives—better coordinate their activities in the field to eliminate gaps and overlap and form partnerships to maximize resources? How might more private sponsors be enrolled, or whole networks of private sponsors activated?

Related to money is the issue of jobs. As more and more citizens at every level of the peacemaking process get involved, and as more and more students are electing peace studies, global studies, and conflict resolution as their career interests, the demand for work in the field grows, but the availability of jobs is severely limited. What career opportunities are those now receiving Ph.D.s in the field being prepared for? Where will they go for experience? This is a particular problem for those interested in international work. On the domestic scene, there are mediation centers and public policy programs in many localities, but internationally, there is virtually nothing available except to go into teaching, a field with limited opportunities.

There are a few support organizations—such as the Peace Studies Association; the Consortium on Peace Research, Education, and Development; the National Conference on Peace Making and Conflict Resolution; and the National Peace Institute Foundation—but these tend to have small administrative staffs. There are a growing but still small number of practitioner groups, and they don't have the resources to hire the numbers of practitioners who are currently in the marketplace. The citizen diplomacy community is beginning to generate a number of organizations, and the development, activist, media, and religious communities all have their professional networks in place, providing some job opportunities. Except for the Ted Koppels and Peter Arnetts who command high salaries, however, the pay tends to be low and the job demands high.

What we are starting to see, in response to the job scarcity, is that people are creating their own work. In some cases, this means starting whole organizations; in others, it means generating specific projects as part of one's work and getting them funded extrainstitutionally. Two organizations that we found, the Tides Foundation and the Center for Psychological Studies in the Nuclear Age, offer an institutional umbrella for such independent projects. Other equally creative forms will inevitably arise as the field develops over the next decade. The internal pressure for work and jobs by people trained and committed will demand it.

Affective Output

All systems have two types of output: productive and affective. They generate both products or concrete results and feelings, needs, and other energies that are released as part of the work but are not necessarily channeled into a tangible product.

We found that the affective output of the Multi-Track Diplomacy system is not commonly discussed within the field, in part because it would require people to be extremely open and vulnerable, exposing deep personal experiences and feelings. This kind of sharing is not a norm in our society in general; in fact, it is considered normatively deviant in many of the subsystems within the field. For example, when General Schwartzkopf spoke of his feelings about sending men to battle, the country was shocked, both by the content of what he said and by the very fact that he said it.

The work of the Multi-Track Diplomacy community involves issues of great human pain and suffering. It is a field with tremendous inherent stress. One can never do enough fast enough, and there are never enough resources to alleviate the anguish of massive numbers of people. What happens with that stress and those unresolved, often unarticulated feelings about the work is an open question. We know that no energy is lost—it goes somewhere. One opportunity for further research would be to consider where and how the stress of the system gets worked out.

One fact that came to light through our interviews is that people forget to take care of themselves. They get so involved with the work that they neglect their bodies (exercise, rest, proper diet), their personal relationships, and their spiritual nourishment. We found very little normative support for this kind of personal replenishment. Although this phenomenon is not unique to this system, it is exacerbated by the need for peacemakers to be at peace themselves.

"Peace begins at home" is a truism in the field; it is easy to say but harder to live. We can talk intellectually about the relationships among individual, family, community, national, and international conflicts, but it is always easier to focus "out there" on some other situation rather than inward on ourselves. We found the Multi-Track Diplomacy field rife with its own internal conflicts—with competitive norms, power struggles, stereotypes and dehumanizing assumptions about one another, ideological battles. Little attention was given to applying the substantial methodologies and wisdom about global peacemaking that exist within the system to individual and interinstitutional conflicts.

The main exception to this is in the religious community. This community is certainly not immune to internal conflict, but those who define their jobs as working with the states of their own hearts seem to be more willing to make conscious connections between inner and outer phenomena. A few individuals and several organizations also make this a conscious focus. By and large, however, the system is oblivious to its own conflict processes and certainly has no systemic vehicles for addressing or managing them.

Implications

The issues named here represent the agenda for the Multi-Track Diplomacy community for the foreseeable future. As world conditions continue to change, so too will the nature and scope of our work. However, these considerations offer us the opportunity for years of study, research, and action. It is hoped that we can all find something here that speaks to our unique concerns. Perhaps something will suggest a direction that makes sense in our particular work or reinforce an idea that might have been calling. The implications for each of us will be different, but the excitement of being on the curl of the wave of the future is available to all.

Notes

1. John McDonald, "Guide for Newcomers to Track Two Diplomacy," Occasional Paper no. 2 (Washington, DC: Institute for Multi-Track Diplomacy, November 1993).

2. "The Battle of the Sexes: Behind the Broad Support for the War, a Gender Gap Lurks," *Washington Post*, February 19, 1991.

3. This phrase is often used in speaking and in writing by Harold Saunders, retired State Department official (see "Resources" for Track Two).

Intrasystemic Relationships

The relationships between the tracks or components of the Multi-Track Diplomacy system lie at the heart of its functioning. The lines of relationship determine pathways of communication, sharing of resources, and opportunities for collaborative action and mutual enrichment. When the relationships are adversarial or undeveloped, of combative or indifferent energies, the system is operating with unfulfilled or distorted potential.

The lodestar in the multi-track configuration is Track One, the government. That is the only part of the system that can conclude formal agreements and treaties with other nations; it is where ultimate decisions are made about war, peace, and the commitment of national resources. Although the other tracks exist independently, and their products and results are useful in and of themselves, much of their work is ultimately about influencing, changing, laying the groundwork for, or reacting to Track One thinking and action.

Track One is not an easy world to influence from the outside. This is one of the main frustrations and tensions within the entire system, as people from all parts of the circle feel impelled to get their particular wisdom through to the decision makers. The doorways into the policymaking world are narrow, and entrance is limited. Important research goes unread by those who could benefit most by it. New ideas and in-depth knowledge about conflict in general and specific conflict situations in particular don't get translated into viable policies. Methodologies for solving problems without force go unused. Information about the effects of certain policies or about the needs of the people on the ground may not be heard by those who make and implement those policies. Trust developed and relationships built between parties don't get transferred to those in a position to institutionalize those improved relationships. In fact,

Track One sometimes feels threatened by the work of the other tracks and closes in on itself to protect its own turf.

These are serious problems. They indicate a bottleneck of resources and information that, if it occurred in a major business, would never be tolerated and would signal an urgent need for reorganization. Because the Multi-Track Diplomacy system doesn't think of itself as a unit, and because no one part of it, including Track One, is making sure that all parts of the system are in working order, this reorganization doesn't happen. The insularity of each of the components—but especially Track One, with its elitist tradition—is also an important factor. Whatever the causes, and they are undoubtedly myriad, the effect is a system handicapped by its own internal barriers, unable to make full use of its potential for addressing issues of great global concern. It is a system operating at partial power.

The doorway to Track One does exist, but access to it seems to be based on who you know. Former government officials who have become part of the think tank or academic communities but still have important contacts in government may have some access, at least to certain levels of policymaking. They also may have access to key opinion makers, the op-ed pages of major newspapers, and the television interview and news show circuit. Certain institutions have developed trusted reputations on the Hill or in the State Department over many years, regardless of the specific individuals involved, so their work might get through to someone. Occasionally someone like Bishop Edmund Browning, presiding bishop of the Episcopal Church, may be heard because of the power of his or her position. For others without personal clout or contact, the door is generally closed.

One natural alliance that exists is between the government and the academic and research communities. Spokespeople for these fields are called to give testimony at congressional hearings and are invited to policy discussions from time to time. One of the think tank community's primary goals is to gain access to policymakers, and it has numerous ways of attempting to do so. However, since Track One is primarily an operational mode and is often crisis oriented, its officials are not likely to sit down and read papers or reports. Therefore, the best access the intellectual community has takes the form of face-to-face meetings, which again means personal contact.

The other natural alliance, albeit an ambiguous one, is between the government and the press. The media, at least mainstream news media, focus their reporting on the actions and activities of Track One. Feature stories may give historical or cultural background or elucidate the plight of the people in a conflict zone, but most of the news about conflict is in relation to what the government does or doesn't do, says or doesn't say.

Government officials have another way of influencing public opinion: by appearing on television news shows or calling press conferences, or even writing editorial pieces for the op-ed pages. In conflict situations, as we saw in Panama, Grenada, the Persian Gulf, Somalia, and Haiti, the government exerts specific controls on the press, limiting access to events and personnel and managing the content and the process of what is sent back to the States. In other words, Track One has a strong grip on the information channels, both passively and actively, and is a primary source for what the public hears about world events and how the understanding of those events is framed.

Track One has a natural adversary within the system, and that is Track Six, the activist community. Much of the work of that component is in direct public protest against the policies of the government, as in antiwar demonstrations or in advocacy of a policy or constituency not favored by the government, such as the work of CISPES (Committee in Solidarity with the People of El Salvador) or the Sanctuary movement. This adversarial relationship, when understood properly, could produce creative possibilities for learning. When understood improperly, it can lead to increased polarization, frustration, and anger.

We saw very little to indicate a willingness by Track One (and even by many in Track Six) to use the natural tension between the two to increase communication and facilitate growth. Most were stuck in the assumption that battle, active or inactive, defined the relationship. Since the power differential is inherently uneven (barring the massive public outpouring that this country witnessed during the Vietnam era or that Eastern Europe witnessed during the fall of the Soviet empire), if there is a battle, Track One will be the "winner." As in all win-lose situations, though, it may be seen to be the loser as well, for by brushing aside or actively intimidating or punishing activists and their concerns, it robs itself of vital resources.

The activist community could be seen as providing a critical function for the larger whole. It questions assumptions on which policies are based and espouses moral and humanitarian criteria for those policies. A systems view would say that the activist community is expressing the fight or oppositional energy of the system, thereby relieving the rest of the system from the task of taking on the government.

The press can be adversarial too in its relationship to the government. Its job is to investigate as well as report; this involves uncovering mismanagement and error and exploring all sides of an issue as well as presenting factual information and the official viewpoint. The press can take a fight-leader role in the system, but it too ultimately suffers from the inequality of power, as witnessed by the limitations placed on the press during the Persian Gulf War.

The media have another important and often overlooked function to play in the peacemaking community. Journalists are frequently posted for several years to areas where there may be ongoing issues of conflict and peace. They get out into the streets, they talk to officials from both sides and to people at all levels of society. They probably know more about what is actually happening on the ground than any embassy staff, certainly more than any State Department official in Washington. Much of this knowledge is background information, used as the basis for daily or weekly articles, but it is precisely that depth of background that should be considered in making major policy decisions. We heard of no circumstances, however, in which this knowledge was tapped by policymakers in any way. This is another example of how the system leaks its energy or loses opportunities for optimum functioning.

In terms of other intrasystemic relationships, we see a clear and natural alliance between academia and professional conflict resolution. Much of the theory building and many of the practitioners in conflict resolution come from the academic community. There is a penetrating relationship, as well, between the religious and the activist communities. In many cases, religious figures are key leaders in activist movements (for example, the Berrigans or Martin Luther King Jr.); in other cases, religious or religion-oriented organizations take significant leadership roles in activist causes (for example, the Fellowship of Reconciliation spearheaded a major "no blood for oil" campaign during the gulf crisis).

There is also some crossover between the citizen involvement field, especially in its international development and international exchange activities, and the activist and faith communities. Many development projects are faith based, and many exchange programs serve activist causes. All activist groups could also be categorized in Track Four, citizen involvement, because their activities are not officially sponsored by public or private institutions but are undertaken by voluntary associations of individuals seeking common cause.

The business community occupies a unique place in the Multi-Track Diplomacy field and is the least visible. It is intimately connected with Track One by virtue of having to deal with U.S. and foreign trade regulations and related personnel. When foreign trade issues are used as part of foreign policy, as they frequently are, the business community is directly affected, as the economic sanctions in South Africa have so clearly demonstrated. American business is also directly affected by conflicts around the world, as in the case of rebuilding the Kuwaiti infrastructure destroyed by war. In addition, businesspeople who have developed strong local contacts are occasionally asked by diplomats to carry informal messages or exert influence on local decision makers.

Business leaders with a political consciousness have also formed groups to relate directly to U.S. foreign policy, sometimes as advocates of particular views, sometimes just to educate themselves. They are often included in think tank programs, working with the intellectual community to provide policy perspectives.

There is also a growing connection between Tracks Four and Six (citizens and activists) and the business community. As individuals and small groups of private citizens become acquainted with people from other countries, they often see opportunities for mutually beneficial business contacts. Many such relationships exist, for instance, in Central America and increasingly in Africa, where Americans are setting up U.S. businesses to help Third World artisans sell their goods here. There is a burst of interest, too, between business and those citizen diplomats involved with the former Soviet Union and Eastern Europe.

Additionally, there is a growing socially conscious section of the business world, often comprising individuals who have a personal history with social activism. These individuals, groups, and networks of businesses are stepping into the arena of peace work in a number of ways: by setting up investment portfolios that give preference to those companies that meet particular environmental or political standards, by investing in Third World projects, by seeking greater U.S. funding for peace-related activities, and by exploring possibilities for economic conversion.

The business community is also integrally involved in the funding world. Many multinational corporations have their own foundations that fund peacemaking and peacebuilding projects. Indeed, much of the money from what we consider to be major foundations originally came from wealthy businesspeople. Individual businessmen and -women outside the main foundation community are also frequent financial supporters of individuals and institutions in all the tracks of the Multi-Track Diplomacy system. This philanthropic activity is not necessarily as visible as that of the foundation world, but it plays a vital role in enabling a good portion of the system to do its work.

The funding community, critical to the success of the entire multi-track world, is, like Track One, a focus of power within the system. A large percentage of the work in the conflict resolution, academic, research, citizen, activist, religious, and media worlds can happen only with outside funding. By controlling the pursestrings, the funding community essentially controls the agenda. Who gets money, how much, and for what activities determine the direction of the whole system. At present there is little coordination among the various key players and different segments of the funding community, or among funders and the multi-track system as a whole. This suggests possibilities for dialogue and cooperation in the future that could change the patterns of funding, and the functioning of the system, dramatically.

Indeed, all the intrasystemic relationships described here are the seedbed for future action. We need not accept that just because groups have traditionally related to one another in certain ways they must continue to do so. We can change our habitual ways of thinking and feeling about one another; we can change our patterns of interaction. In our family lives, we work hard to have good relations not just with our immediate families but with our extended circles as well, with our aunts and uncles, cousins and grandparents. So too in the Multi-Track Diplomacy family, we can make an effort to establish harmonious relationships. Just as family members help one another, so too can the tracks of the multi-track system watch out for one another and offer help, guidance, and combined effort.

Relationships take work to develop, nurture, and maintain. Who will take responsibility for improving the relationships within this system? Who will look for ways to build on what works and deconstruct what doesn't, so that new forms might arise through which we can be more effective as a system? These are some of the questions and challenges facing us as we approach a new century. The growing awareness of our interdependence assures us that the fact of relatedness is a given; the variables have to do only with the quality of those relationships.

Recommendations

The results of the research presented in this book will be interpreted differently by each reader. Many conclusions and suggestions are embedded in its various sections. We have drawn up a series of twelve conclusions and recommendations as a way of gathering together the many lessons of this work and expressing the essence of our challenge. We see this challenge as a wonderful opportunity, an invitation to action. We are all invited by this work to:

1. *Take a systems view.* Start to think of ourselves, whatever part we play, as part of the circle that makes up the whole Multi-Track Diplomacy system. Know that each point on the circumference of the circle is just as important to the whole as any other but cannot exist and function alone. Become more sensitive to the interactions we have, or don't have, with other parts of the system—with thoughts, assumptions, ideas, feelings, lack of knowledge, and fantasies we hold about other parts of the whole. Remind ourselves and our colleagues regularly that the work we are doing is of great interest to others. Use the term *Multi-Track Diplomacy* or some similar phrase to keep the context of the whole in mind. Find common ground, seek a common vision, with other parts of the system.

2. *Build relationships.* Network, connect, communicate, collaborate, cooperate, build coalitions. Find new ways to reach across the invisible lines of the nine tracks to share, learn, and act together. Seek out new and unusual partnerships or combinations; include the marginalized; invite participation from the unexpected; reach out to those who seem different, even antagonistic, to see what we can learn from and share with one another. Practice the art of making the strange familiar.

Reach out across national and cultural boundaries, building and nourishing relationships with our colleagues in other parts of the world. Things happen through personal connections and through networking; "it's all in who you know" is a true working principle. The person we meet today may tomorrow become a head of state, a foundation president, an anchor on a news show, or a deep and lasting friend. Consciously build networks, introducing people to one another, catalyzing joint ventures. Sustain and enhance these relationships over time.

3. *Work with our internal conflicts.* Acknowledge the elitism, stereotypes, aggressiveness, and competitiveness that pervade our work environment, our conscious or unconscious thinking, our patterns of behavior. Actively seek win-win resolutions of differences. Embrace and utilize state-of-the-art methodologies and human technologies for internal peacemaking; request help from those who are skilled in that work to facilitate the process. Realize that armed conflict in the world is one expression of humanity's collective anger and unresolved pain. When we resolve or heal our own wounds, we energize the healing mode for all. Practicing conflict resolution with ourselves and with one another is an act of generosity.

4. *Create work models that reflect the vision.* See the internal system as a mirror of the external world and deal with the same issues inside as outside—individually, intraorganizationally, and interorganizationally. Know that the medium is the message, that the process or means cannot be different from the content or ends. If we seek to build a world of peace, we must build it also within our own system. The issues "out there" are the same issues we must address—not just intellectually, but practically—in our structures, our activities, our relationships. Develop ways of working with one another that address our ethnocentricity; strengthen our ethnic, racial, and gender diversity; demonstrate cross-disciplinary approaches; model collaboration and partnership; experiment with new forms of power sharing; and honor our interdependence and the whole range of human experience, thought, and emotion.

5. *Create new resources.* Be innovative in finding new sources of funding, in enhancing the effectiveness of traditional sources. Help the funding community become better coordinated, and bring the resources of the business community more solidly into the field. Explore and encourage international multi-track funding coalitions, private sponsorships, and funding networks. Be creative and unwavering in discovering and supporting ways to make sure that the whole system and each of its parts have all they need to operate successfully and to flourish. Step beyond competition and realize that we create new resources when we work together.

6. *Share our knowledge.* Generate formats to transfer and translate our knowledge, wisdom, skills, experience, methodologies, and questions across systemic lines. Convene multi-track study groups, conferences, computer networking, seminars, and action projects; bring people from the different tracks together as a matter of course to look at substantive and process issues. We need multi-track forums on specific conflicts, on ethics, on reconciliation and forgiveness, on improving funding and jobs, on training needs for the twenty-first century, on the theory and practice of conflict resolution, on issues of emerging democracies, on understanding the dynamics of identity-group conflict and change agentry. Any subject that is part of the Multi-Track Diplomacy agenda is an appropriate topic to pursue from a multi-track perspective.

7. *Explore systemic peacemaking.* Explore the possibilities of coordinating peacemaking processes among the different tracks. What would it look like if the players from the religious community, the conflict resolution experts, the official diplomats, and the citizen diplomats who were involved in a particular peace process talked with one another about what they were doing? They could even plan their activities to enhance one another's interventions as much as possible, even coordinate a vision and a plan of action. What could be the opportunities and the benefits of this approach?

8. *Create multi-track institutions.* Develop organizations, centers, institutes, programs, and projects that take the multi-track perspective, that address issues that affect the whole system, that convene multi-track events, that evaluate and service the needs of the system. Especially, create bodies that address leadership development and multidisciplinary, multiethnic training.

9. *Work to legitimate the field.* Act at every level to embed in humanity's collective mind the understanding that force is not the way to solve our problems; that a whole network of peacemaking and conflict resolution specialists exists with methodologies and technologies that can be successful in addressing our gravest global concerns. Activate our vast collective network around the world to educate the decision makers, the opinion makers, the media, the public, the various constituencies of the different tracks about the power and potential of peacemaking as a tool of international, intergroup relations, and about the critical need to incorporate this approach into our policies and our actions. Encourage the development of special institutions—regional and transnational—to serve as conflict resolution centers with a humanitarian rather than a political mode,

so that any groups in conflict anywhere in the world, regardless of resources, political standing, and military or economic might, can get the help they need to resolve their conflicts.

10. *Take care of ourselves.* Learn to deal with the stress of the work more overtly, to share and transform the pain, the fear, the doubt, the hopelessness, and the suffering of ourselves and of those we aim to assist in moving from conflict to peace. Give ourselves and one another permission to talk about how it feels to do the work we do. Find ways of relaxing the body, calming the mind, and inspiring the heart. Make the giving and receiving of nourishment at every level a norm of the system to counteract the work's tendency to be depleting and discouraging.

11. *Take responsibility.* Realize that no one is going to do all these things for us. We have to step forward and do what needs to be done. Track One needs to open its doors to the wealth inherent in the rest of the system. Meanwhile, the rest of us must keep knocking. The funding community needs to take a more systemic view, be innovative, and expand its horizons and resources. The rest of us can develop creative funding alternatives. The business community needs to come forward more openly and make its extensive resources available to the system. We can encourage and invite specific businesses to do so. In other words, although each component has its own work to do, others can encourage and stimulate that work in various ways. We don't need to play victim and pretend that our hands are tied because someone else isn't doing what we want.

12. *Realize our power.* We live in a moment ripe with global change and transformation. Collectively we hold much of the information and skill to facilitate that change, to bring the world more gracefully and less painfully through the difficult times we face. Although any one action on the part of any one of us may seem like a drop in the bucket, given the dire needs of the people on this planet, it is the many drops that will eventually fill the bucket to overflowing. The information is indeed in the membership. We have all we need to be successful at our task if we do not shrink from the opportunities to use that collective power for the good of the whole.

We are the hope for the world's future.

Bibliography

This bibliography lists books and articles that are relevant references to one, some, or all of the nine tracks of the Multi-Track Diplomacy system. The reader should note that there are important references not listed here that are produced internally by most of the organizations listed previously in this book under "Resources," including internal annual reports, newsletters, and other publications. For more information, contact the organizations directly.

Books

Avruch, Kevin, Peter W. Black, and Joseph A. Scimecca, eds. *Conflict Resolution: Cross-Cultural Perspectives.* New York: Greenwood Press, 1991.

Azar, Edward E. *The Management of Protracted Social Conflict: Theory and Cases.* Brookfield, VT: Gower, 1990.

Azar, Edward E., and John W. Burton, eds. *International Conflict Resolution: Theory and Practice.* Sussex, England: Wheatsheaf, 1986.

Barnaby, Frank, ed. *The Gaia Peace Atlas: Survival in the Third Millennium.* New York: Doubleday, 1988.

Bendahmane, Diane B., and John W. McDonald. *Perspectives on Negotiations: Four Case Studies and Interpretations.* Washington, DC: U.S. Department of State, Center for the Study of Foreign Affairs, 1986.

Benjamin, Medea, and Andrea Freedman. *Bridging the Global Gap: A Handbook to Linking Citizens of the First and Third Worlds.* Washington, DC: Seven Locks Press, 1989.

Brock-Utne, Birgit. *Educating for Peace: A Feminist Perspective.* The Athene Series. New York: Pergamon Press, 1985.

Brown, Seyom. *The Causes and Prevention of War.* New York: St. Martin's Press, 1987.

Brown, Sheryl J., and Kimber M. Schraub, eds. *Resolving Third World Conflict: Challenges for a New Era.* Washington, DC: United States Institute of Peace Press, 1992.

Burch, Wileta, and James Burch et al. *Everything Has Changed.* Palo Alto, CA: Beyond War, 1989.

Burton, John. *Deviance, Terrorism and War: The Process of Solving Unsolved Social and Political Problems.* Canberra, Australia: Australian National University Press, 1979.

———. *Resolving Deep Rooted Conflict: A Handbook.* Lanham, MD: University Press of America, 1987.

———. *Conflict: Resolution and Prevention.* New York: St. Martin's Press, 1990.

———, ed. *Conflict: Human Needs Theory.* New York: St. Martin's Press, 1990.

Burton, John, and Frank Dukes. *Conflict: Practices in Management, Settlement and Resolution.* New York: St. Martin's Press, 1990.

———, eds. *Conflict: Readings in Management and Resolution.* New York: St. Martin's Press, 1990.

Camus, Albert. *Neither Victims nor Executioners.* New York: Continuum, 1980.

Clark, Mary. *Ariadne's Thread: The Search for New Modes of Thinking.* New York: St. Martin's Press, 1989.

Clements, Kevin P. *UN Peace Keeping at the Cross Roads.* Christchurch, New Zealand: ANU Press, 1993.

———. *Building International Community.* London, England: Allen and Unwin, 1994.

———, ed. *Peace and Security in the Asia Pacific Region.* Tokyo: United Nations University Press, 1993.

Cohen, Raymond. *Negotiating across Cultures: Communication Obstacles in International Diplomacy.* Washington, DC: United States Institute of Peace Press, 1991.

Coser, Lewis. *The Functions of Social Conflict.* New York: Free Press, 1956.

Cranna, Michael. *The True Cost of Conflict: Seven Recent Wars and Their Effects on Society.* New York: New Press, 1994.

Cromartie, Michael, ed. *Peace Betrayed? Essays on Pacifism and Politics.* Washington, DC: Ethics and Public Policy Center, 1989.

Cruikshank, Jeffrey, and Lawrence Susskind. *Breaking the Impasse: Consensual Approaches to Resolving Public Disputes.* New York: Basic Books, 1988.

Crum, Thomas F. *The Magic of Conflict: Turning a Life of Work into a Work of Art.* New York: Simon and Schuster, 1987.

Doob, Leonard W. *The Pursuit of Peace.* Westport, CT: Greenwood Press, 1981.

———, ed. *Conflict Resolution in Africa: The Fermeda Workshop.* New Haven, CT: Yale University Press, 1970.

Enloe, Cynthia H. *Ethnic Conflict and Political Development.* Lanham, MD: University Press of America, 1986.

First Steps to Peace: A Resource Guide. New York: Joel Brooke Memorial Committee of the Fund for Peace, 1985.

Fisher, Roger, and William Ury. *Getting to Yes: Negotiating Agreement without Giving In.* 2d ed. New York: Penguin Books, 1991.

Fisher, Ronald J. *The Social Psychology of Intergroup and International Conflict Resolution.* New York: Springer-Verlag, 1990.

Garrison, Jim, and John-Francis Phipps. *The New Diplomats, Citizens as Ambassadors for Peace.* London: Green Books, 1989.

Geyer, Alan. *The Idea of Disarmament!* Elgin, IL: Brethren Press; Washington, DC: Churches' Center for Theology and Public Policy, 1982.

Gromyko, Anatoly, and Martin Hellman. *Breakthrough/Emerging New Thinking: Soviet and Western Scholars Issue a Challenge to Build a World beyond War.* New York: Walker and Co., 1988.

Gurr, Ted R. *Why Men Rebel.* Princeton, NJ: Princeton University Press, 1970.

Habib, Philip C. *Diplomacy and the Search for Peace in the Middle East.* Washington, DC: Institute for the Study of Diplomacy, Georgetown University, 1987.

Hollins, Harry B., et al. *The Conquest of War: Alternative Strategies for Global Security.* Boulder, CO: Westview Press, 1989.

Horowitz, Donald L. *Ethnic Groups in Conflict.* Berkeley: University of California Press, 1985.

Iklé, Fred Charles. *Every War Must End.* Rev. ed. New York: Columbia University Press, 1991.

Isaacs, Harold R. *Idols of the Tribe: Group Identity and Political Change.* Cambridge, MA: Harvard University Press, 1989.

Jack, Homer A., with Masamichi Kamiya. *World Religion/World Peace.* New York: World Conference on Religion and Peace, 1979.

Jensen, Ros. *Max: A Biography of C. Maxwell Stanley, Engineer, Businessman, World Citizen.* Ames: Iowa State University Press, 1990.

Kahn, Lynn Sandra. *Peacemaking: A Systems Approach to Conflict Management.* New York: University Press of America, 1988.

Klare, Michael T., and Daniel C. Thomas, eds. *Peace and World Order Studies, a Curriculum Guide.* 5th ed. Five College Program in Peace and World Security Studies. Boulder, CO: Westview Press, 1989.

Kriesberg, Louis. *The Sociology of Social Conflicts.* Englewood Cliffs, NJ: Prentice-Hall, 1973.

———. *International Conflict Resolution: The U.S.-USSR and Middle East Cases.* New Haven, CT: Yale University Press, 1992.

Kriesberg, Louis, Terrell A. Northrup, and Stuart J. Thorson, eds. *Intractable Conflicts and Their Transformation.* Syracuse, NY: Syracuse University Press, 1989.

Kriesberg, Louis, and Stuart Thorson, eds. *The Timing and De-escalation of International Conflicts.* Syracuse, NY: Syracuse University Press, 1991.

Lakey, George. *Power Peacemaking: A Strategy for a Living Revolution.* Philadelphia: New Society Publishers, 1987.

Lederach, John Paul. *Preparing for Peace: Conflict Transformation across Cultures.* Syracuse, NY: Syracuse University Press, 1995.

McDonald, John W., and Diane B. Bendahmane. *Conflict Resolution: Track Two Diplomacy.* Rev. ed. Washington, DC: Institute for Multi-Track Diplomacy, 1995.

McLaughlin, Corinne, and Gordon Davidson. *Spiritual Politics: Changing the World from the Inside Out.* New York: Ballantine Books, 1994.

Mitchell, Christopher R. *The Structure of International Conflict.* London: Macmillan, 1981.

———. *Handbook on the Problem-Solving Approach.* London: Frances Pinter, 1996.

Montville, Joseph V., ed. *Conflict and Peacemaking in Multi-Ethnic Societies.* Lexington, MA: Lexington Books, 1990.

Moore, Christopher W. *The Mediation Process: Practical Strategies for Resolving Conflict.* San Francisco: Jossey-Bass, 1986.

Newsom, David D. *The Diplomacy of Human Rights*. Washington, DC: Institute for the Study of Diplomacy, Georgetown University, 1986.

————. *Private Diplomacy with the Soviet Union*. New York: University of America Press, 1987.

North, Robert C. *War, Peace, Survival: Global Politics and Conceptual Synthesis*. Boulder, CO: Westview Press, 1990.

Peace and World Security Studies. *Guide to Careers, Internships & Graduate Education in Peace Studies*. Amherst, MA: Five College Program in Peace and World Security Studies, 1990.

Peringer, Christine, ed. *How We Work for Peace*. Dundas, Ontario: Peace Research Institute, 1987.

Popper, David H., ed. *Adapting American Diplomacy to the Demands of the 1990s*. Washington, DC: American Academy of Diplomacy, 1989.

Prospects for Conflict or Peace in Central and Eastern Europe: Report of a Study Group, May 1990. Washington, DC: United States Institute of Peace, 1990.

Sandole, Dennis, and Hugo van der Merwe, eds. *Conflict Resolution Theory and Practice: Integration and Application*. New York: Manchester University Press, 1993.

Saunders, Harold H. *The Other Walls: The Arab-Israeli Peace Process in a Global Perspective*. Princeton, NJ: Princeton University Press, 1991.

Schindler, Craig, and Gary Lapid. *The Great Turning*. Santa Fe, NM: Bear & Co., 1989.

Schrag, Philip G. *Listening for the Bomb: A Study in Nuclear Arms Control Verification Policy*. Westview Special Studies in National Security and Defense Policy. Boulder, CO: Westview Press, 1989.

Shuman, Michael, and Gale Warner. *Citizen Diplomats*. New York: Continuum, 1987.

Simpson, Dick. *The Politics of Compassion and Transformation*. Athens: Ohio University Press, 1989.

Simpson, Smith. *Perspectives on the Study of Diplomacy*. Washington, DC: Institute for the Study of Diplomacy, Georgetown University, 1986.

Thompson, W. Scott, et al., eds. *Approaches to Peace: An Intellectual Map*. Washington, DC: United States Institute of Peace Press, 1991.

United Nations. *The International Day of Peace*. New York: United Nations, 1989.

Volkan, Vamik D. *The Need to Have Enemies and Allies: From Clinical Practice to International Relationships*. Northvale, NJ: Jason Aronson, 1988.

Volkan, V. D., J. V. Montville, and D. A. Julius, eds. *The Psychodynamics of International Relationships*. Vol. 1, *Concepts and Theories*; Vol. 2, *Unofficial Diplomacies at Work*. Lexington, MA: Lexington Books, 1990.

Weeks, Dudley. *Conflict Partnership: How to Deal Effectively with Conflicts*. Orange, CA: Trans World Productions, 1984.

Weiss, Thomas G., ed. *The United Nations in Conflict Management: American, Soviet and Third World Views*. New York: International Peace Academy, 1990.

Whittemore, Hank. *CNN: The Inside Story*. Boston: Little, Brown, 1990.

Worchel, S., and W. G. Austin, eds. *Psychology of Intergroup Relations*. 2d ed. Chicago: Nelson Hall, 1986.

Ywahoo, Dhyani. *Voices of Our Ancestors: Wisdom Teachings from the Cherokee Fire*. Boston: Shambhala, 1987.

Articles, Chapters, and Occasional Papers

Barnes, Bruce E. "The French Nuclear Tests in the South Pacific: Case Study of an International Environmental Dispute." PRC Working Paper Series no. 1987-7. Honolulu: Program on Conflict Resolution, University of Hawaii, 1987.

Barnes, Craig. "Beyond the Cold War: The Demand for a New World View." Making a Decision about War Series. Palo Alto, CA: Beyond War Foundation, July 1988.

Barrett, Robert C. "Grantmaking in Negotiation, Collaborative Problem-solving, and Conflict Resolution." William and Flora Hewlett Foundation, December 1989.

Bernards, Reena. "Dialogue Conference between Jewish and Palestinian American Women." Summary report. Stony Point, NY, 1989.

Boulding, Elise. "Image and Action in Peace Building." *Journal of Social Issues* 44, no. 2 (1988): 17–37.

Buchanan, Robert. "The Road to the Summit: Oxfam America's Advocacy for Famine Relief in Ethiopia." Unpublished paper, October 1990.

Burton, John. "Conflict Resolution as a Political System." Working Paper 1. Fairfax, VA: Center for Conflict Analysis and Resolution, George Mason University, 1988.

Chasin, Richard, and Margaret Herzig. "Family System Therapy and Soviet-American Relations: Modes of Analysis and Intervention." Working paper. Cambridge, MA: Center for Psychological Studies in the Nuclear Age, 1988.

Crocker, Chester A. "Conflict Resolution in the Third World: The Role of Superpowers." Paper for United States Institute of Peace Conference, Washington, DC, 1990.

Davies, John L., and Charles N. Alexander. "Alleviating Political Violence through Enhancing Coherence in Collective Consciousness: Impact Assessment of the Lebanon War." Paper presented to the 85th annual meeting of the American Political Science Association, Atlanta, GA, September 1989.

Diamond, Louise. "Peacemakers in a War Zone." Occasional Paper no. 1. Washington, DC: Institute for Multi-Track Diplomacy, November 1993.

———. "Beyond Win/Win: The Heroic Journey of Conflict Transformation." Occasional Paper no. 4. Washington, DC: Institute for Multi-Track Diplomacy, November 1994.

Fisher, Ronald J. "Third Party Consultation as a Method of Intergroup Conflict Resolution." *Journal of Conflict Resolution* 27, no. 2 (June 1983): 301–34.

———. "Needs Theory, Social Identity and an Eclectic Model of Conflict." In *Conflict: Human Needs Theory*, ed. John Burton, pp. 89–112. New York: St. Martin's Press, 1990.

———. "Third Party Consultation: A Problem-Solving Approach for De-escalating International Conflict." Unpublished paper, Saskatoon, Canada, 1993.

Fisher, Ronald J., and Loraleigh Keashley. "The Potential Complementarity of Mediation and Consultation within a Contingency Model of Third Party Intervention." *Journal of Peace Research* 28 (1991): 29–42.

Galtung, Johan. "Violence, Peace, and Peace Research." *Journal of Peace Research* 3 (1969): 167–91.

Geyer, Alan. "Historical Contexts and Ethical Judgments in U.S.-Soviet Relations." Paper presented at the American Society of Christian Ethics, January 1990.

Grant, James P. "The World's Religions for the World's Children." Address to the World Conference on Religion and Peace Conference, Princeton, NJ, July 1990.

Groom, A. J. R. "Paradigms in Conflict: The Strategist, the Conflict Researcher, and the Peace Researcher." In *Conflict: Readings in Management and Resolution*, ed. John W. Burton and Frank Dukes, pp. 71–98. New York: St. Martin's Press.

Harrison, Selig S. "Paths to Peace in Afghanistan: The Geneva Accords and After." Occasional Papers on Peacekeeping no. 1. New York: International Peace Academy, 1989.

"The Helsinki 2000 Appeal, Realizing the Impossible through Citizen Participation—Working Document." Palo Alto, CA: Beyond War, June 1990.

Henderson, Michael. "Moral Re-armament . . . A Factor in World Affairs." Speech given at an International Community Forum presented by Mt. Hood Community College and the Gresham Area Chamber of Commerce, January 1981.

Jack, Homer A., with Masamichi Kamiya. "Stopping the Spread of Nuclear Weapons: The Politics of the Fourth Review Conference of the Non-Proliferation Treaty." WCRP report. New York: World Conference on Religion and Peace, September 1990.

Jolna, Stacy. "Waging Peace; CNN Reports on the Global Battle against War." *TBS Transponder* 2 (September 1989). Atlanta, GA: Turner Cable Network Sales.

Kay, Alan F. "The Value of Serial Polling: Techniques and Examples of the Use and Benefit of Serial Polling to Better Understand Public Opinion Observed in the Americans Talk Security (ATS) Series of Twelve National Surveys, October 1987 through September 1988." Winchester, MA, November 29, 1989.

————. "Americans Talk Security Series of National Telephone Surveys (ATS) from October 1987 through March 1990: The Military Budget and Public Opinion." Winchester, MA, April 17, 1990.

Kelman, Herbert C. "The Problem-Solving Workshop in Conflict Resolution." In *Communication in International Politics*, ed. Robert Merrit, pp. 168–204. Urbana: University of Illinois Press, 1972.

————. "Interactive Problem-Solving: A Social-Psychological Approach to Conflict Resolution." In *Dialogue toward Inter-Faith Understanding*, ed. W. Klassen. Tantur, Jerusalem: Ecumenical Institute for Theological Research, 1986.

————. "The Political Psychology of the Israeli-Palestinian Conflict: How Can We Overcome the Barriers to a Negotiated Solution." Presidential address, International Society of Political Psychology, Amsterdam, 1986.

————. "Informal Mediation by the Scholar/Practitioner." In *Mediation in International Relations: Multiple Approaches to Conflict Management*, ed. J. Bercovitch and J. Rubin, pp. 64–96. London: Macmillan, 1992.

Kelman, Herbert C., and Stephen P. Cohen. "The Problem-Solving Workshop: A Social-Psychological Contribution to the Resolution of International Conflicts." *Journal of Peace Research* 13 (1976): 79–90.

————. "Resolution of International Conflict: An Interactional Approach." In *Psychology of Intergroup Relations*, ed. Stephen Worchel and William G. Austin, pp. 323–42. Chicago: Neison Hall, 1986.

"Kingian Nonviolence Vocabulary." Atlanta: Martin Luther King Jr. Center for Nonviolent Social Change, 1989.

Kriesberg, Louis. "Peace Movements and Government Peace Efforts." *Research in Social Movements, Conflicts and Change* 10 (1988).

Laue, James H. "Getting to the Table: Creating the Forum for Negotiations in Deep-Rooted Conflict." Bonn: Stresemann Institute, 1989.

————. "The Emergence and Institutionalization of Third-Party Roles in Conflict." In *Conflict: Readings in Management and Resolution*, ed. John W. Burton and Frank Dukes, pp. 256–72. New York: St. Martin's Press, 1990.

Laue, James H., and Gerald W. Cormick. "The Ethics of Intervention in Community Disputes." In *The Ethics of Social Intervention*, ed. Gordon Bermant, Herbert Kelman, and Donald Warwick, pp. 205–32. New York: Halsted Press, 1978.

Laue, James H., et al. "Getting to the Table: Three Paths." *Mediation Quarterly* 20 (Summer 1988): 7–18.

Lederach, John Paul, and Paul Wehr. "Mediating Conflict in Central America." *Journal of Peace Research* 28 (1991): 85–98.

Liu, F. T. "United Nations Peacekeeping: Management and Operations." Occasional Papers on Peacekeeping no. 4. New York: International Peace Academy, 1989.

McDonald, John W. "Global Environmental Negotiation: The 1972 Stockholm Conference and Lessons for the Future." Project on Multi-Lateral Negotiations, 1989.

————. "Further Exploration of Track Two Diplomacy." In *The Timing and De-escalation of International Conflicts*, ed. Louis Kriesberg and Stuart Thorson, pp. 201–20. Syracuse, NY: Syracuse University Press, 1991.

————. "Guidelines for Newcomers to Track Two Diplomacy." Occasional Paper no. 2. Washington, DC: Institute for Multi-Track Diplomacy, November 1993.

————. "How to Be a Delegate: International Conference Diplomacy." Occasional Paper no. 3. Washington, DC: Institute for Multi-Track Diplomacy, March 1994.

"A Message and Resolution on the Gulf and Middle East Crisis Adopted by the General Board." National Council of the Churches of Christ in the U.S.A., November 15, 1990.

Mills, Susan R. "The Financing of United Nations Peacekeeping Operations, the Need for a Sound Financial Basis." Occasional Papers on Peacekeeping no. 3. New York: International Peace Academy, 1989.

Montville, Joseph V. "Ethnic Conflict Resolution in the Soviet Union: The Heritage of Stalin." Esalen Institute Conference, November 1990.

————. "Transnationalism and the Role of Track Two Diplomacy." In *Approaches to Peace: An Intellectual Map*, ed. W. Scott Thompson and Kenneth M. Jensen, with Richard N. Smith and Kimber M. Schraub, pp. 253–69. Washington, DC: United States Institute of Peace, 1990.

————. "The Healing Function in Political Conflict Resolution." In *Conflict Resolution Theory and Practice: Integration and Application*, ed. Dennis J. D. Sandole and Hugo van der Merwe, pp. 112–28. Manchester, England: Manchester University Press, 1993.

Montville, Joseph V., and William D. Davidson. "Foreign Policy According to Freud." *Foreign Policy* 45 (Winter 1981–82): 145–57.

Müller, Robert. "Acceptance Speech." UNESCO Peace Education Prize, Paris, 1989.

————. "A Copernican Framework for Philanthropy (Love for Humanity) and Gaiaphily (Love for the Planet)." Unpublished paper, 1989.

Notter, James. "Trust and Conflict Transformation." Occasional Paper no. 5. Washington, DC: Institute for Multi-Track Diplomacy, April 1995.

Oxfam America. "Against All Odds: Perspectives for Peace in Kampuchea." Oxfam America policy report, 1989.

Papp, Daniel S., with John Diehl. "The United Nations: Issues of Peace & Conflict." Atlanta, GA: Southern Center for International Studies, 1989.

Pickus, Robert. "Professions, Peace and Politics: Defining a Responsible Organizational Engagement." In *Building the Professional Dimension of Educational Exchange*, ed. Joy M. Reid. Yarmouth, ME: Intercultural Press, 1988.

Potapchuk, William, and Chris Carlson. "Using Conflict Analysis to Determine Intervention Techniques." *Mediation Quarterly* 16 (Summer 1987): 31–43.

Program on Conflict Resolution. "Researching Disputes across Cultures and Institutions." A research report of the Program on Conflict Resolution, University of Hawaii, Honolulu, 1990.

Richeson, Donna, and Virginia Willcox. "Understanding Central America." Making a Decision about War Series. Palo Alto, CA: Beyond War Foundation, November 1987.

Rikhye, Indar Jit. "The Future of PeaceKeeping." Occasional Papers on Peacekeeping no. 2. New York: International Peace Academy, 1989.

Rothman, Jay. "A Pre-Negotiation Model: Theory and Training, Project on Pre-Negotiation Summary." Policy Studies no. 40, Leonard Davis Institute for International Relations, Hebrew University, Jerusalem, 1990.

Rubenstein, Richard. "Working Paper 2. Group Violence in America." Fairfax, VA: Center for Conflict Analysis and Resolution, George Mason University, 1988.

Sandole, Dennis J. D. "Paradigms, Theories, and Metaphors in Conflict and Conflict Resolution: Coherence or Confusion?" In *Conflict Resolution Theory and Practice: Integration and Application*, ed. Dennis J. D. Sandole and Hugo van der Merwe, pp. 3–24. Manchester, England: Manchester University Press, 1993.

Saunders, Harold H. "Negotiations in a Larger Political Framework." In *International Conflict Resolution: Seven Perspectives*, pp. 3–10. San Francisco: World Affairs Council of Northern California, 1990.

————. "Officials and Citizens in International Relationships." In *The Psychodynamics of International Relationships*, ed. V. F. Volkan, D. Julius, and J. V. Montville, pp. 41–69. Lexington, MA: Lexington Books, 1990.

Saunders, Harold H., and Gennady I. Chufrin. "A Public Peace Process." *Negotiation Journal: On the Process of Dispute Settlement* 9, no. 2 (April 1993): 155–77.

Saunders, Harold H., and Randa Slim. "Dialogue to Change Conflictual Relationships." In *Higher Education Exchange*, pp. 43–56. Dayton, OH: Kettering Foundation, 1994.

Touval, Saadia, and William I. Zartman. "Mediation: The Role of Third-Party Diplomacy and Informal Peacemaking." United States Institute of Peace Conference, Washington, DC, 1990.

United Nations. "Towards Peace in Cambodia." New York: United Nations Department of Public Information, 1990.

———. "The U.N. Role in the Central American Peace Process." New York: Department of Public Information, United Nations, 1990.

United States Institute of Peace. "The Gulf Crisis: Finding a Peaceful Solution." A special report of the United States Institute of Peace, Washington, DC, 1990.

UN Regional Conference for the Non-Governmental Community. "Global Security in the 1980s—The Role of the United Nations in Conflict Resolution, Peacekeeping and Disarmament." New York: Department of Public Information, United Nations, 1986.

U.S. Chamber of Commerce. "Activities of the Center for International Private Enterprise to the Subcommittee on International Operations of the House Committee on Foreign Affairs." July 1990.

"U.S. Policy in the Persian Gulf." Hearings before Committee on Foreign Relations, U.S. Senate, September 5, 20, and October 17, 1990. Washington, DC: U.S. Government Printing Office, 1990.

———. Hearings before Committee on Foreign Relations, U.S. Senate, December 4, 5, 1990. Washington, DC: U.S. Government Printing Office, 1990.

———. Hearings before Committee on Foreign Relations, U.S. Senate, December 6, 12, 13, 1990. Washington, DC: U.S. Government Printing Office, 1990.

van Walt, Michael, and Catherine Ingram. "Unrepresented Nations and Peoples Organization." Unpublished paper, December 1990.

Index

academia. *See* higher education; Track Five
Academy of American Diplomacy, 145
ACCESS, 109
activism. *See* Track Six
advocacy groups, 61, 62. *See also* Track Four; Track Six
Africa, 3, 23, 30, 31, 56, 132, 134, 136, 141, 160
age, representation in Multi-Track Diplomacy communities, 41, 88, 148
Agency for International Development, U.S., 33
Albert Einstein Institution, 79–80
alternative dispute resolution (ADR), 3
American Academy of Diplomacy, 33
American Friends Service Committee, 98, 102. *See also* Quakers
American University, 145–46
Amnesty International, 87, 91, 93
anger, actions based on, 88, 92
antinuclear programs, 90, 109, 138
Antioch College, 75
Arab-Israeli relations. *See* Middle East
Arca Foundation, 113–14
arms (weapons), 134, 135; control, 131, 135, 138; nuclear, 90, 110, 134, 138
Arnetts, Samuel, 153
Austrian Peace Institute, 30

Baha'i International Community, 97, 102
Barton, Robert, 114
Benton Foundation, 114
Berrigan, Daniel, 159
Berrigan, Philip, 159
Bolling, Landrum, 8, 43
Bosnia, 30, 31
Boulding, Elise, 75
Brickner, Rabbi Balfour, 103
Brookings Institute, 75–76
Browning, Edmund, 157

Buddhist community, 97, 101
bureaucracy, 27–28, 71–72, 109, 112, 133
Burlington/Puerto Cabezas Sister City Program, 65
Burton, John, 43
Bush, George, 24, 28, 91, 131
business. *See* Track Three
Business for Peace in Iowa, 55
Business for Social Responsibility, 57

caretaking role, 9–10, 99
Carnegie Commission on Preventing Deadly Conflict, 76
Carnegie Corporation, 108, 114
Carnegie Endowment for International Peace, 76
Carter, Jimmy, 43, 143
Catholic community, 97, 101, 105
CDR (Communication/Decisions/Results) Associates, 44, 145
Center for Citizen Initiatives, 65
Center for Defense Information, 76
Center for International Development and Conflict Management, 76–77
Center for International Policy, 77
Center for International Private Enterprise, 57
Center for International Understanding (CIU), 44
Center for Media and Public Affairs, 127
Center for National Policy, 77
Center for National Security Negotiations, 77
Center for Psychological Studies in the Nuclear Age, 153
Center for Psychology and Social Change, 77–78
Center for Strategic and International Studies, 78
Center for Teaching Peace, 78
Central America, 23, 62, 98, 101, 132, 134, 160

change agent process, 141, 146
children, programs on peacemaking and
    world order, 2–5, 71–73, 136
Church of the Brethren, 100
CIA (Central Intelligence Agency), 28
CISPES (Committee in Solidarity with
    the People of El Salvador), 93, 158
citizen diplomacy, 2, 60, 61–62. See also
    private citizens; Track Four
class, social, 61, 63, 74, 121
Clements, Kevin P., 44
Clergy and Laity Concerned, 103, 148
cliquishness. See exclusivity
CNN (Cable News Network), 120, 125,
    127, 140
Coca-Cola Co., 57–58
Cold War, 3, 64, 110, 134, 135, 138
collective action, 55, 88–89, 131–32, 134
collective consciousness, 23–24
colleges and universities. See higher edu-
    cation; Track Five
Colosi, Tom, 45
commerce. See Track Three
Common Ground Productions, 127–28
communication, 2, 7–8, 13, 31, 37, 112;
    between Tracks One and Six, 158;
    Track Three's role in, 52, 57. See also
    media; Track Nine
community, 53–54, 72, 99
Community Nonviolence Resource
    Center, 78
compassion, 39, 88, 97, 99
Compton Foundation, Inc., 114
computers, 122, 126; networks, 121, 123
conflict(s), 13, 17–18, 52, 123, 124,
    133–34; intranational, 3–4, 23, 31,
    133–34; research on, 73, 112, 139;
    Track Six witnessing during, 90
Conflict Management Group, 44–45
ConflictNet, 123
Conflict Research Consortium, 78–79
conflict resolution, 2–3, 13, 74, 123, 132,
    136, 164–65; as an aim of Track Seven,
    97; funding for, 73, 110, 112; legit-
    imization of, 31, 136; not seen as news-
    worthy, 124; provided by Track One,
    26; provided unofficially by Track
    Seven, 100; questions on modes of,
    149–50; as skill needed in Track Six,
    90; studies in academic community,
    71, 73, 142–43; Track Nine's task
    regarding, 120; Track Seven activities
    in, 99; Track Three's task in, 52, 56;
    training in, 30, 70–71, 138. See also
    Track Two

Conflict Resolution Catalysts, 45
Conflict Resolution Center International,
    79
Congress, U.S., 27, 28–29, 144
consciousness, 6, 100; collective, 23–24;
    maharishi field theory of, 98; social, 53,
    54, 160
conservativism, 53, 121
Consortium of Peace Research, Educa-
    tion and Development (COPRED), 19,
    71, 79, 153
contrition, 40, 99
cooperative action, Track Six reliance on,
    88–89
corporate works of mercy, 99
Council on Foundations, 109, 114–15
creativity, 27, 111–12
credibility, as issue in Multi-Track
    Diplomacy, 18, 41, 142–44, 151
Crocker, Chester A., 34
cross-cultural relationships and training,
    53–54, 62, 70

Dartmouth Conference, 138
Davidson, Gordon, 106
decision making, 17–18, 31, 109, 120,
    126, 131, fig. 15
Defense Department, U.S., 28
defense industries, 56, 135, 140
de Klerk, Frederik W., 17
democratization, 61, 63, 110, 132–33. See
    also Track Four
demonstration projects, use by Track
    Two, 42
demonstrations (protests), 89, 92, 99,
    133, 136, 140, 158
developing nations (Third World), 52,
    53–55, 56, 101, 147, 160. See also Africa;
    Central America; South America
development, economic and social,
    12–13, 17, 30, 60–62, 131, 138; Track
    Seven activities in, 99–100, 101. See also
    Track Four
Diamond, Louise, 45
Diehl, Jackson, 128
Diomedes, Inc., 58
diplomacy, 4, 26–36; definitions of,
    11–12, 26. See also Track One
diversity, 41, 55, 88, 131–32, 147–50. See
    also ethnic groups; gender; identity
    groups; race

Eastern Europe, 23, 24, 62, 136, 158, 160;
    challenges for Track Three, 55, 56;
    democratization, 132

Eastern Mennonite University Master's Program in Conflict Analysis and Transformation, 79, 145–46
EcoNet, 123
economics, 7, 52, 54, 56, 110, 121; globalization of, 22, 136–37. *See also* development
ecumenism, 97, 99–100, 102
education, 2–5, 13–16, 53, 70–86, 145
   activity of other tracks, 39, 89–90, 99; Track Four, 60, 62, 63–64
   higher. *See* higher education
   Institute of Peace support for, 19
   K-12 programs, 2–5, 71–73, 136
   use of the media, 120, 121
   See also Track Five
Educators for Social Responsibility, 62
election monitoring, UN, 30
electronic communications media, 120, 121, 122, 123–24
elitism, 126, 163; of Track One, 30, 33, 42, 157. *See also* exclusivity
emotions: expressed in Track Six community, 88; involved in Multi-Track Diplomacy, 154–55
empowerment, 3, 54, 109, 110, 133; mutual, as aim of Track Two, 37, 38; Track Four activities in, 62, 63, 64; Track Six activities in, 90
environmental issues, 3, 12, 22, 55, 131–32, 137, 140; included in security studies, 110; involvement of socially conscious businesses, 54; programs funded by progressive foundations, 109; as a Track Six concern, 87, 88, 90, 91
Esalen Institute, 65
ethics. *See* moral issues
ethnic groups, 132; conflicts, 3–4, 23, 31, 74, 91, 133–34; representation in Multi-Track Diplomacy community, 61, 88, 109, 147–48. *See also* race
European Community, 131
European Union, 32
Evangelical Protestant community, 97, 101
exchange programs. *See* citizen diplomacy; Track Four
exclusivity (cliquishness), as issue in Multi-Track Diplomacy, 18, 28, 33, 102, 121. *See also* elitism

faith in action, 5, 97–107. *See also* Track Seven
fax machines, 122, 124

feedback, 9, 29
Fellowship of Reconciliation, 103, 159
filmmaking community, funding for, 152
Fisher, Roger, 46
Fisher, Ron, 46
Five College Program in Peace and World Security Studies, 12–13, 80
Ford Foundation, 108, 115
foreign policy, U.S., 54, 90, 151, 160. *See also* policymakers; Track One
forgiveness, 40, 99
Foundation for a Global Community, 46, 103
foundations, 108–19, 138, 150–53
Fourth Freedom Forum, 58
Fuller, Robert, 65
funding, 5, 108–19, 122, 143, 150–54; as major challenge for Track Two, 41; for Track Six, 87–88, 90. *See also* Track Eight
Funds for Peace, 115

game theory, 132, 158
gender
   differences in perspectives on war and violence, 147–48
   representation in Multi-Track Diplomacy community, 61, 71, 88, 109, 121, 147–48; in Track One, 28; in Track Seven, 99; in Track Three, 53, 55; in Track Two, 41
General Agreement on Tariffs and Trade, 32
General Service Foundation, 115
geo-economics, 32, 56
geopolitics, 134, 136
George Mason University, 145–46
Geyer, Alan, 104
Global Business Network, 58
global village phenomenon, 22, 124
government: in Multi-Track Diplomacy, 4, 26–36; in "One Track, Two Track" model, 2, 3. *See also* Track One
grants, from foundations, 110, 112, 153
grassroots community, 138; funding for, 108–9, 110, 151; Track Four's approach, 60, 62, 63, 64; Track Six connections with, 87–88, 89, 92
"Guide for Newcomers to Track Two Diplomacy" (McDonald), 146
Gutlove, Paula, 46

Hammer, Armand, 138
Harvard Negotiation Project, 80, 145–46

health issues, 22, 53, 110
Hewlett (William and Flora) Foundation,
  73, 115–16
  higher education, 2–5, 20, 24, 42
  peace and conflict resolution studies,
    142–43, 153
  peacemaking programs, 70–73, 123
  personnel, 17, 72, 122; former govern-
    ment officials as, 157; Track Two
    professionals from, 39
  training for Track One and Track Two
    professionals, 145–46
  See also Track Five
Hindu community, 97
humanitarianism, 71–72, 88
humanity, unity of for Track Seven, 97,
  102
human rights, 8, 12, 17, 30, 87, 90
Human Rights Watch, 93–94

identity groups, 24, 26, 31, 37, 55, 132,
  149; conflicts, 3, 23, 133–34, 139. See
  also diversity; ethnic groups
IDR (International Dispute Resolution)
  Associates, 46–47
IF, 94
Institute for Conflict Analysis and
  Resolution, 80
Institute for Global Communications,
  123–24, 128
Institute for International Economics, 81
Institute for Multi-Track Diplomacy
  Professional Development Program, 81,
  145
Institute for Resource and Security
  Studies, 81
Institute for the Study of Diplomacy, 35,
  81
Institute of World Affairs, 81–82
InterAction (American Council for
  Voluntary International Action), 66
international business. See Track Three
International Business Diplomacy
  Program, 58–59
International Conference of Peace
  Institutes (June, 1990), 14–16
International Monetary Fund (IMF),
  35–36
International Negotiations Network, 43,
  139
International Peace Academy, 82
International Peace Research
  Association, 19, 71, 82
international politics, 21, 23–24, 30, 53;
  and diplomacy, 26–33

International Society of Political
  Psychology, 19
International Studies Association, 19
intranational conflicts, 3–4, 23, 31,
  133–34
Iowa Peace Institute, 66, 71, 144
Israeli-Arab relations. See Middle East

Jewish community, 97–98, 101
Jewish Peace Fellowship, 104
Johns Hopkins University: School of
  Advanced International Studies, 145
Joint Chiefs of Staff, U.S., 28
Josey Bass Inc., Publishers, 128
justice, 12–13, 73, 87–88, 97, 99; funding
  for programs and studies, 109, 110
just war theory, 100

Kelman, Herbert C., 47
Kennedy. Kathleen, 146
Kettering Foundation, 109
King, Martin Luther, Jr., 99, 159
Konoderkeka, Arthur, 8
Koppel, Ted, 140, 153
K-12 programs on peacemaking and
  world order, 2–5, 71–73, 136
Kriesberg, Louis, 47
Kumarian Press, 128–29
Kuwait, 91, 160. See also Persian Gulf War

language: diplomatic, 27, 28; as an issue
  for Track Two, 41
leadership, 9, 101; development, 62, 72
Lederach, John Paul, 47
Legacy International, 66
Lewis, Samuel, 144
liberation theology, 98, 101
Lincoln, Bill, 48
Lloyd, Robert, 94
lobbying, 41, 89
lose-lose situation, 132

MacArthur (John D. and Catherine T.)
  Foundation, 108, 116
McCarthy, Coleman, 129
McDonald, John, 146
McDonald, John W., 48–49
McKnight Foundation, 111, 116
maharishi field theory of consciousness,
  98
Maharishi International University, 104
market economics, 54, 56; global, 136–37
Marks, Susan Collins, 48
Martin Luther King Jr. Center for
  Nonviolent Social Change, 104

McLaughlin, Corinne, 106
media, 17, 120–26, 157–58. *See also* Track
    Nine
mediation, 26, 73, 99, 150; as an activity
    of Track Two, 38–39, 40; taught in
    schools, 70, 73, 136
Mennonite Central Committee (MCC),
    104–5
Mennonites, 97, 100
Middle East, 3, 56, 62, 101, 133, 135, 141
militarism, 13, 87
military, the, 6, 20
Miller, Aaron, 35
Mitchell, Christopher, 49
MIT-Harvard Public Disputes Program,
    82–83
Montville, Joseph V., 1, 49
moral issues (ethics), 41, 145–46, 148;
    importance in Track Seven, 97,
    100–101; Track Six based on, 87, 88
Moral Re-Armament, Inc. (MRA), 105
Mott (Charles Stewart) Foundation, 108,
    116–17
Mugabe, Robert, 8
Muller, Robert, 35
multinational corporations, 52, 53–55,
    160–61
Multi-Track Diplomacy, 1, 9, 11–25, 126;
    defined, 4–5; external issues, 131–41;
    internal issues, 141–55; intrasystemic
    relationships, 156–61; professional
    development, 144–47; systems analysis,
    5–10. *See also individual tracks*
Muslim community, 98
Muste (A. J.) Memorial Institute, 117

Nangle, Joe, 105
National Association for Mediation in
    Education, 71, 73, 83
National Conference of Peace Making
    and Conflict Resolution (NCPCR), 19,
    153
National Democratic Institute, 111
National Endowment for Democracy, 111
National Institute for Dispute Resolution,
    83
National Peace Institute Foundation,
    83–84, 153
National Security Council, 28–29
nation-states, 26, 37, 132
Native Americans, 97, 101
NATO (North Atlantic Treaty
    Organization), 32, 136
natural law, 101
negative peace, defined, 12

negotiation, 26, 29, 31, 126, 131, 149
networking/networks, 7–8, 39, 54, 89,
    162–63; computers, 121, 123; estab-
    lished by Track Seven, 100, 144; fund-
    ing, 113; by news reporters, 125. *See also*
    relationships
NETWORKS: A National Catholic Social
    Justice Lobby, 105
New Age, 97
news reporting, 17, 121, 124–26, 157–58.
    See also television; Track Nine
nongovernmental diplomacy/profes-
    sional conflict resolution, 4, 37–51; in
    Track Two of "One Track, Two Track"
    model, 1–2. *See also* Track Two
nongovernmental organizations, 2–4,
    60–61, 100. *See also Track Two; Track
    Four; Track Six; Track Seven*
nonviolence, 12, 31, 73, 99, 100, 124, 140;
    commitment to, 88, 135–36
Non-Violence International, 66–67
North American Free Trade Agreement,
    132
NTL Institute of Behavioral Science, 84,
    148
nuclear weapons, 90, 110, 134, 138

Oklahoma City federal building bomb-
    ing, 136
Organization of American States, 34–35
Organization of Security and
    Cooperation in Europe, 32
Overseas Development Council, 67
Oxfam America, 67

pacifism, 12, 99, 100. *See also* nonvio-
    lence
Partners for Democratic Change (PDC),
    49
Pathways to Peace, 59
Pax World Service, 67
peace: definitions of, 12–13; as a "soft"
    science in academia, 71; studies of, 123,
    142–43
Peace Action (formerly San/Freeze), 87,
    94
Peace and Conflict Resolution Studies
    Program, 84
Peace and Justice Center, 94–95
peacebuilding, 1–2, 13, 141, 150–51
Peace Corps, 67
Peace Development Fund, 117
peace institutes, 144
peacekeeping, 13, 16, 30
Peacelinks, 68

peacemaking, 2–4, 20–21, 131, 138
  defined, 13
  internal, 163
  legitimization of as international rela-
    tions tool, 136, 142–44, 164
  Multi-Track Diplomacy model, 4–10,
    141. See also Multi-Track Diplomacy;
    individual tracks
  "Track One, Track Two" (two-track sys-
    tem) model, 1–2
PeaceNet, 123
Peace Studies Association, 19, 71, 84, 153
peer mediation, 70, 73
Persian Gulf War, 6, 20, 31, 91, 92, 143;
  news coverage, 125–26, 159
Pew Charitable Trust, 108, 117
philanthropy, 5, 108–9, 150, 161. See also
  Track Eight
Physicians for Social Responsibility, 62,
  68, 149
Ploughshares Fund, 108, 117
policymakers, 13, 89; access to, 156–60;
  education of, 42, 60, 62–63. See also foreign policy; Track One
political action, as method for Track Six,
  87
"politically correct" thinking, 90
politics, 13, 23–24, 132–33; power, 26, 30,
  37, 38, 149; Track Seven's involvement
  in issues, 100, 101. See also international
  politics
positive peace, defined, 12–13
poverty, 13, 52, 99
power, 23–24, 26, 29, 42, 134–36, 165
  abuse of, 88; Track One's potential for,
    33
  disparities in, 40, 91, 158
  at grassroots level, 60
  political, 26, 30, 37, 38, 149
  through association, 18
  of Track Eight in Multi-Track
    Diplomacy
    system, 113
Primacov, Evgeny, 8
private citizens, 144–45; empowerment
  of, 109, 133; observance of suffering,
  17; Track Six community as, 87, 89. See
  also Track Four
private voluntary organizations, 61, 62.
  See also Track Four
problem solving, 37, 55, 56, 131, 150;
  workshops, 38, 39, 40
pro bono work, 151
professional interest groups, 61, 62, 149.
  See also Track Four

profits, orientation to, of mainstream
  business community, 52, 53
Program on International Conflict Analysis and Resolution (PICAR), 49–50
Protestants, Evangelical, 97, 101
Protestants, mainstream, 97, 100
protests (demonstrations), 89, 92, 99,
  133, 136, 140, 158
psychological issues, 7, 40, 139
Psychologists for Social Responsibility, 62
public, the, 30, 55, 89, 126, fig. 15; education of, 42, 60
Public Broadcasting Service (PBS), 123,
  126
Public Information, UN Department of,
  34
public opinion, 20, 120–21, 126
public policy issues, 108, 110, 121
Pugwash Conference, 138

Quakers, 8, 97–98, 100, 102

race, representation in Multi-Track
  Diplomacy community, 41, 61, 88, 99,
  109, 121, 147–48; in Track One, 28; in
  Track Three, 53, 55
rallies, 89, 99
Reardon, Betty, 12–13
reconciliation, 13, 97, 99
refugees, 90, 100
relationships, 2, 7–8, 29, 110, 162–63;
  building of, 37, 40, 52, 53–54, 60, 89.
  See also networking
relief work, 62, 63, 99
Religious Action Center, 105–6
religious community: in Multi-Track
  Diplomacy, 5, 97–107; in "One Track,
  Two Track" model, 2. See also Track
  Seven
religious groups (identity groups), 26;
  conflicts, 3, 23, 74
research. See education; Track Five
Research Center of War, Peace, and the
  News Media, 129
Resolving Conflict Creativity Program,
  84–85
Resource Center for Nonviolence, 95
Rockefeller Foundation, 117–18
Rothman, Jay, 50
Rubins, James, 129
Russian-American Center, 68
Rwanda, 31, 134, 136

Sage Publications, 129
Said, Abdul Aziz, 50

St. Martin's Press, 130
San Fuentes, Vince, 34
satellite technology, 123, 126, 140
Saunders, Harold, 23, 24, 50
School for International Training, 85
Schwartzkopf, Norman, 154
science, 21–22, 62, 131–32
Scott, Molly, 95
Search for Common Ground, 48, 123
security, 32, 138; studies of, 108, 110, 111, 123
Security Council, UN, 3, 20, 30
self-consciousness, 7, 8–9
Simpson, Smith, 11
Smith, Alec, 8
Smith, Ian, 8
social systems, analysis of, 6–10
Society of Professionals in Dispute Resolution, 19, 85
Soka Gakkai International-USA, 106
Somalia, 30, 31, 136
South Africa, 3, 56, 141
South America, 62, 98, 101, 132, 134
South Dakota Peace and Justice Center, 95
Southern Center for International Studies, 85
sovereignty, 32, 132
Soviet Union, former, 132, 160; citizen visits to and exchanges with, 61–62, 64, 138
space bridges, 121, 124, 140
Spark M. Matsunaga Institute for Peace, 82
spirituality, 97, 99–100, 101
Stanley Foundation, 85, 109
State Department, U.S., 27, 28–29, 140, 145
Stoner Broadcasting System, 59
stress, 17–18, 63, 154, 165
suffering, 17–18, 101, 165; observance of, 17–18, 63, 154–55; relief of, 99, 101–2
Sunray Mediation Society, 106
Syracuse University, 145–46

television, 121, 122, 123–26, 157, 158
terrorism, 134, 140
think tanks, 20, 70–72, 89, 122, 157, 160; alliances with Track One, 142; funding for, 152; with religious perspective, 97–98. *See also* Track Five
Third World. *See* developing nations
Threshold Foundation, 108, 118
Tides Foundation, 108, 118, 153

Track Eight in Multi-Track Diplomacy (funding), 5, 108–19, 138, 150–54, 163, *fig.* 15; focus on security studies, 138; relations with other tracks, 142, 160–61. *See also* funding
Track Five in Multi-Track Diplomacy (education community), 4–5, 70–86, 137–39, *fig.* 15; alliances with other tracks, 142, 157, 159; funding for, 108, 110, 151, 152, 153. *See also* education
Track Four in Multi-Track Diplomacy (private citizens), 4, 11, 24, 60–69, 138, 146, *fig.* 15; electronic communications field arising from, 122; exchange programs provided by international business, 54; foundation funding for, 110; during the Persian Gulf War, 20; relations with other tracks, 88–89, 159–60, 160; staffs and boards of progressive foundations drawn from, 109; time given to in news media, 122. *See also* private citizens
Track Nine in Multi-Track Diplomacy (communication; media), 5, 11, 20, 22, 120–30, 146, *fig.* 15; commentary in as a Track Seven activity, 99; creative use by Track Two, 41; funding for, 110, 153; relationship with Track One, 157–58, 159; role in forming views on the Persian Gulf War, 6–7; role in Track Five activities, 72, 74; Track Four activities in, 62, 64. *See also* communication; media
"Track One, Track Two" model of peacemaking, 1–2
Track One in Multi-Track Diplomacy (diplomatic community; government), 4, 11, 20, 26–36, 133, 156–60, *fig.* 15; alliances with think tanks, 142; commentary from in news media, 122; constructive debates within, 149; operational responsibility, 74; relations with other tracks, 42, 64, 72, 90–92, 121, 143; search for wealthy donors, 151; terrorism as subject for discussion, 140; tuned to public opinion as expressed through the media, 120
Track Seven in Multi-Track Diplomacy (religious community), 5, 12, 17, 97–107, 138, 146, *fig.* 15; credibility as problem for, 144; funding for, 152, 153; minimal internal conflict, 155; peace churches in Protestant tradition, 100–101; relations with other tracks, 19, 63, 88, 142; time given to in news media, 122; visible role in issues of war and peace, 140

Track Six in Multi-Track Diplomacy (activist community), 5, 14–16, 17, 87–96, 137, 146; credibility as problem for, 144; funding for, 110, 152, 153; relations with other tracks, 19, 142, 158–60; staffs and boards of progressive foundations drawn from, 109; time given to in news media, 122; Track Seven's similarities, 99

Track Three in Multi-Track Diplomacy (business community), 4, 11, 12, 20, 52–59, 146, *fig.* 15; conversion of defense industry to non-defense manufacturing, 135, 140; credibility as problem for, 144; funding for, 88, 113, 152; multinational corporations, 52, 53–55, 160–61; personnel as resource for Track Five, 72; relations with other tracks, 62, 160–61; search for new markets, 138–39; shielded from direct experience of suffering, 17; staffs and boards of foundations drawn from, 109; Track Six community outlets, 90

Track Two in Multi-Track Diplomacy (nongovernmental professional conflict resolution community), 4, 11, 17, 37–51, 123, 139–40, 145–46, *fig.* 15; constructive debates within, 149; funding for, 110, 112, 152, 153; generational issue acute in, 148; legitimacy sought by, 41–42, 143–44; during the Persian Gulf War, 20; pro bono work, 151; relations with other tracks, 64, 142, 143, 159; terrorism as subject for discussion, 140. *See also* conflict resolution

Track Two in "Track One, Track Two" model, 1–2

trade policies, 54, 56, 132

training. *See* education; Track Five

TransAfrica, 68

20/20 Vision, 68–69

Unitarian Universalist United Nations Office, 106

United Nations, 3, 20, 27, 29–30, 31–32, 34, 36, 100, 133, 136

United Nations Institute for Training and Research (UNITAR), 30

United States Institute of Peace, 18–19,

86, 111, 118, 144

universities. *See* higher education

values, 17
in Multi-Track Diplomacy community, 27, 39, 61, 109, 122; of Track Seven, 98–99; of Track Six, 88–90
stressed in school programs, 71–72

VCRs/video, 121, 123

Vietnam War, 12

violence, 3, 12–13, 56, 73, 88, 134–36; differing perspectives on, 147–48; seen as newsworthy, 124; structural, 13, 74, 135. *See also* conflict(s)

Volkan, Vamik D., 51

W. Alton Jones Foundation, 116

war, 3, 20–21, 26, 147–48. *See also* conflict(s)

Washington Peace Center, 87, 95

Washington Post (newspaper), 126, 147–48

weapons. *See* arms

Weeks, Dudley, 51

Weston Priory, 107

Westview Press, 130

"whole body politic," 149

win-lose situation, 132, 158

Winston Foundation for World Peace, 109, 111, 119

win-win situation, 132

Witness for Peace, 95–96

witnessing, as a Track Six activity, 89, 90

Working Assets Funding Service, 119

World Conference on Religion and Peace, 107

world (global) order, 11, 21–24, 33, 70, 131, 132

World Orders Models Project, 86

World Policy Institute, 86

World Trade Center bombing, 136

World Trade Organization, 32, 132

worldview(s), 37, 74, 90, 112, 131, 135; transformation of, 21–24, 100

World War II, 12

World Without War Council, 19, 86

Yugoslavia, former, 30, 31, 133–34, 136

Zimbabwe (Rhodesia), 8